GW01606106

# Memoirs of a Hunter

## Experiences in Finland and Russia 1904-1930

# Memoirs of a Hunter

## Experiences in Finland and Russia 1904-1930

**Friedrich Remmler**

**Translated by Ingmar Remmler**
**Edited by Martin Hollinshead**
**Illustrations by Vadim Gorbatov**

**The Fernhill Press**
*Staffordshire*

First published in the UK in 2009 by
The Fernhill Press, Staffordshire.
Reprinted 2012



ISBN 978-0-9563169-0-5

# Contents

# Acknowledgements

Several people helped bring this book to print. Key to the project was Ingmar Remmler, who not only found the manuscript to begin with but acted as translator, freeing me to concentrate on the editing side of things. Vadim Gorbatov's help was massively appreciated and the importance of his work – totally and utterly unique – cannot be overstated. Jevgeni Shergalin and Kuno Seitz were ready to field numerous questions, and David Horobin cast a critical eye over the finished manuscript and was also willing to pull on the proof-reader's cap. The book was finally passed to Paul Morgan for a last read through before publication. As with previous projects, my wife Tonya was involved throughout: from the first rough draft to finally watching the whole thing cross the finish line, her support was invaluable.

Martin Hollinshead

# Editor's Introduction

A multi-lingual hunter, trapper, eagle falconer, horseman, filmmaker, author, and holding a PhD in chemistry, Friedrich Wilhelm Remmler lived a life so full it strained at the seams. One of three children, he was born in Finland in 1888. His father was German, his mother Swedish. He grew up on the north shore of Lake Ladoga in what was then eastern Finland (Karelia), today Russia, where his father owned an iron mine, but he also spent time in Helsinki attending school and university.

After World War I he and his younger brother moved to central Finland and founded a zoological station that shipped animals to zoos all over Europe. His brother eventually tired of the operation, but Remmler continued with it until the outbreak of World War II.

Through all of this, and bagging his first hare at just six years old, Remmler was an obsessive hunter, pursuing fox, lynx, wolf, hare and various game birds. Central to this hunting were his hounds (primarily the Finnish stövare) and while he occasionally kept gun dogs, hounds provided him with most of his sport. It was hound work far removed from foxhunting or beagling: there was no pack and no following a pursuit across country. Instead, a lone hound or single couple would be released to push the quarry along its run, bringing it, hopefully, to the hunter. It was a patient waiting game, the quarry's habit of running a circular escape route being relied upon totally.

Remmler will always be best known for his work with golden eagles. Acquiring his first bird at just fifteen, Remmler's eagle falconry was not only unique for Finland, it was pretty much unique for all Europe. The golden eagle had always been a bird of Central Asian falconry and while a few Europeans had experimented with them, Remmler was the first to achieve proper success. This alone would have guaranteed him a place in falconry history, but what really has him standing alone is where his hawking eventually ended up – wolves. Remmler not only took Asia's most formidable hunting bird, he also took its most formidable quarry.

Remmler's passion for hunting and hawking saw him travel a great deal, his family's wealth and influential contacts opening doors into worlds almost beyond comprehension: a business contact in St. Petersburg brought invitations to massively elaborate hunting events with borzois and between 1904 and 1914 there were yearly trips out to the Kirghiz Steppe to hawk wolves with native eagle falconers.

What makes these experiences all the more fabulous is that they are never to be repeated: the great borzoi kennels were lost with the Russian Revolution and the eagle falconry Remmler knew would go too, only hanging on further east to eventually become the overexposed tourist spectacle of today. Even much of the hunting he enjoyed in Finland has been relegated to history, each foray, each strapping on of skis, taking Remmler through times and places vanished forever. This is what makes his story so fascinating – so valuable. And so intriguing, for until very recently the fact that he had recorded any of it was completely unknown.

The discovery of Remmler's account was pure chance. In 2007 his youngest son, seventy-eight-year-old Ingmar, was deep in the cellar of his Ontario farmhouse searching for old photos. The previous year I'd explored the falconry side of his father's life in a little volume entitled *The last Wolf Hawker* and was now planning a follow-up article. We'd been in regular contact since the publication of the book and he and his brother Orvar were continuing to help me with my ongoing research.

Well, photos Ingmar did find. But that's not all. Blowing the dust of a box that had lain in his cellar for thirty-five years, he discovered something else – a lost manuscript! Written in German, the manuscript had been completed in April 1972 and immediately submitted to a large publishing house in Germany. Remmler's covering letter was still with it – as was their polite refusal. It was his only attempt to get it published. A few months later he was dead.

Within two weeks I had a copy of the manuscript in front of me. Its packaging eagerly ripped off, I was initially a little disappointed in that it contained a huge amount of falconry material already published by Germany's oldest falconry club, the Deutscher Falkenorden, and the North American Falconers' Association. I had also drawn heavily from the same material in *The last Wolf Hawker*. However, as I continued to read, it soon became clear that it also held a massive amount of totally new text on hunting and trapping – a side of Remmler's life about which very little was known.

There was no question that this new material should be published and so it was decided to translate, edit and restructure the manuscript to produce a book that included some falconry – Remmler's first trip to the Kirghiz Steppe – but focussed mainly on the hunting and trapping. Which is exactly what we did: Ingmar handled the translation and I took responsibility for the other work.

With the book now carrying the title *Memoirs of a Hunter*, as editor and publisher I was very excited about the text but still saw a big problem – we had no illustrations. A few photos had been discovered with the manuscript, but they didn't enhance the writing and were clearly re-enactments of earlier events. We needed illustrations and I saw only one artist, the incredible Vadim Gorbatov of Moscow. To read Remmler's account was to immediately see Vadim's work, his ability to so convincingly take the observer back through time, matching him perfectly to the book. Vadim had helped me with projects before: in 1995 he'd supplied a dramatic cover painting for my book *Hawking with Golden Eagles* and together we'd also produced some of his falconry work as limited edition prints. I knew he was too busy to undertake work specifically for the book, but I'd seen a couple of his paintings that were so close to the text they could have indeed been commissioned. Might he have more?

I described the book – the type of hunting and the period involved – and told him I'd be grateful for anything he could let me have. Two weeks later a CD arrived that left me open mouthed. It was as if artist and author had travelled through the experiences together. This wasn't luck; words and art had been waiting for each other. It was all there, capercaillie, bears and wolves all sliding straight into their specific chapters. Some portions of text couldn't be illustrated. But Remmler would forgive this: after thirty-five years of gathering dust, his words were going to be sprinkled with magic to finally live. Turn the page and as the clock rolls back 105 years join him as he begins his tale.

# 1

# An Evening in St. Petersburg

It was August 1904 and we were seated in the outdoor theatre of the St. Petersburg Aquarium – an entertainment park known to all who visited the capital during the time of the Tsars. The stage at the Aquarium always attracted a more select audience than that of the Zoological Garden, where in place of tables and chairs, seating was in the form of simple wooden benches.

Visits to the Aquarium were common. My father was a German mining engineer who had emigrated to Finland and established an iron mine on the north shore of Lake Ladoga, in what was then eastern Finland, now Russia. The ore from the mine was shipped down the lake to the Putislov Works in St. Petersburg and we often joined a consignment to enjoy the sights and entertainment. In fact St. Petersburg was practically a second home, visits only being curtailed during the colder months when the lake froze.

Evenings at the Aquarium were always lively affairs, with incredible amounts of caviar and champagne being consumed – the less well off making do with dill pickles and sour herrings washed down with vodka. On this particular evening things were livelier than ever. A few weeks earlier the Russian far-eastern fleet had been destroyed by the

Japanese as it tried to break out of Port Arthur. It was the second of two disasters. Just before this, the pride of the Russian navy, the battleship Petropavlovsk, had been lost. It was the sinking of this great ship that was now being re-enacted on the stage. The ship's deck was before us, with noisily exploding grenades raining down on it. Now and again the ship's cannons would spew fire and ear-splitting thunder, but there was no sign of the crew, who were perhaps to be imagined sheltering below decks.

Suddenly the grenades stopped and the admiral appeared topside. Swinging his sabre wildly he yelled, 'I'll scuttle the ship myself!' From the audience there was little reaction, but it proved no empty threat, for no sooner had he disappeared below decks than a devastating explosion sent glasses rattling as the ship was engulfed in an enormous cloud of smoke. When this eventually cleared, a big hole could be seen in the deck, and as the waves – reams of blue silken cloth – rose higher and higher, the mighty Petropavlovsk was swallowed. Down she went, sparing not so much as a mouse.

Our host, Neratov, chief director of the Putislov Works, had either witnessed the spectacle before or simply wasn't interested. His back was to the stage the whole time; not even the massive explosion caused him to turn around. He was engrossed in telling my father about his plans to construct a rail network across his vast estates in the Lower Don. My father commented that he'd be better off mechanising the harvest, thus saving seventy men the need to manually handle the grain. But Neratov only responded, 'What would I do with the lazy devils then? Let them stand and watch!'

Also at our table was Neratov's right hand man Lisizin, Schuschin the office manager at my father's mine, and my twelve-year-old brother, Hans.

On the stage the tone was now somewhat lighter, the poor admiral having been replaced by thirty or so scantily clad dancing girls. My brother and I were captivated – until the conversation at our table turned to my hawking, a topic not even this visual distraction could compete with!

The previous year I'd acquired a young male golden eagle – Odin –

and, although only fifteen, I'd managed to train him and fly him to mountain hare and fox. For the family it was a source of great novelty and pride. Without mentor or books to guide me I'd become Finland's only falconer, the sport being totally unknown in my homeland. I'd been inspired by my uncle. He was working in oil production at the Caspian Sea and also drilling out on the Kirghiz Steppe. The latter location brought him into direct contact with native eagle falconers and he'd sent back tales that had me desperate to own my own eagle.

It was my uncle that was now being discussed.

'During the Christmas holidays Friedrich is going to join the Kazakhs for some wolf hawking on the Kirghiz Steppe. It's been arranged by his uncle, head of operations at Nobels.'

'Oh, the Swede,' said Neratov. 'I hear he's the right man to handle that pack of Tartars down there! Well, if the lad's going to be out that way, why doesn't he head north after the hawking and join me for the winter wolf hunt at my lodge in the Urals.'

Like my father, Neratov was a passionate hunter and the amount of money he devoted to this distraction was astonishing: with an army of staff, a massive array of hunting dogs and several vast estates and hunting lodges, nothing could have matched the intensity and glamour of it all. The winter wolf hunt involved his greatest passion of all: borzois. This was a time – before the revolution – that saw the use of these great hounds restricted to the nobility and those of the highest social standing. They were a statement, a possession of the greatest value; they were hounds bred to perfection to not only look magnificent but to be lethal in the field. Run at hare and fox, wolves were their ultimate quarry. It was a fabulous and extravagant type of hunting the revolution would bring to an end; the great kennels would be broken up and many of the hounds destroyed.

I had never seen Neratov's borzois in action – never seen a living borzoi – and looked at my father, desperate for him to agree to the invitation. I could see the offer had taken him by surprise: he was well aware of how colourful such gatherings could be, with vodka flowing in rivers. Nevertheless, it would have been impossible to turn Neratov down.

# 2
# The Kirghiz Steppe

Three months later my adventure began. At that time the Kirghiz Steppe was closed to travellers and only accessible by special permit. With mine arranged through one of my father's contacts, a few days before the end of school I climbed aboard the Helsinki to St. Petersburg train to begin my four-day rail journey to Orenburg.

In Viborg two Russian officers and their wives boarded the train and settled themselves in my compartment. They were a dull bunch, staring silently into space most of the time.

At the border station of Terijoki – a two-hour journey made an eternity in such company – a halt was scheduled and most passengers swiftly made their way to the station restaurant. My companions were more eager than most and the reason for their haste was soon clear. In the middle of a serving table was a pyramid-like contraption made up of five layers of wooden boards. Each board contained numerous holes, into which nestled glasses of vodka. Next to the pyramid stood a tub of pickled gherkins and a basket of forks.

The officers and their wives dashed forwards as if their very lives depended upon it, spiking a gherkin with one hand and grabbing a glass of vodka with the other. Immediately they were in a gherkin and vodka frenzy, the eye hardly able to follow the speed at which both were consumed. I knew Russians were highly skilled in the art of consuming vodka, but I'd never seen anything like this – especially from officers' wives.

All returned to the train in various stages of drunkenness and with the silent sombre mood of earlier now a distant memory, I was provided with entertainment of the liveliest and most vociferous nature. There were stories, songs and wild theatrical outbursts. It was all most revealing. Indeed, by the time we arrived at the Finnish station in St. Petersburg I probably knew more about them than their mothers!

The rail line between St. Petersburg and Moscow runs straight as an arrow except for three small curves. Legend tells that when the line was originally planned, it zigzagged from town to town. When this proposal was presented to the Tsar, it didn't suit him at all and he immediately took a ruler and drew a straight line between St. Petersburg and Moscow. However, three of his fingers extended over the ruler resulting in three small bumps, which his engineers followed when the line was laid. Who knows if the story is true, but without it the curves make no sense at all.

On the Moscow train I shared my sleeping berth with three travellers from England. Every evening before going to bed, each of these gentlemen would carefully empty his purse onto the compartment's small table, count its contents and then make neat little coin stacks. In the morning the money was once again counted and put away. This happened each evening without fail. Having an upper berth, I was sorely tempted to make a clumsy nighttime exit and scatter their precious coins everywhere. It would have been worth it just to watch the argument over the recount.

Early on day five the train pulled into Orenburg. At that time the rail link to Tashkent was still under construction and would not be in full service until 1905. Sufficient track had been laid to enable travellers to cover several hundred kilometres but it was a totally hit and miss affair with no timetable at all. However, I was in luck. The stationmaster assured me that a work train would be leaving next morning and I would be able to hitch a ride south. This little delay suited me perfectly. I'd heard about Orenburg's fascinating Eagle Market, now I had the chance to see it for myself.

About twenty sleighs were lined up outside the station, each

Orenburg was a hawk-trading town of great historical significance, golden eagles changing hands alongside hawks and falcons. The men involved were not only expert trappers but also famous for their falconry skills and were often employed as hawk trainers by those buying birds.

manned by a huge bear-like driver. Russian sleigh drivers and coachmen were always great bulky men. It was a kind of tradition – expected. And if the necessary bulk was lacking, layers of clothing and heavy overcoats gave the desired effect. Sitting behind one of these giants was to travel with no forward view at all. His great width – taking up the entire driver's bench – blotted out the horse completely, unless travelling by a three-horse troika in which case only the middle animal was lost.

I walked along the row of sleighs calling, 'Eagle Market, Eagle Market.' And immediately all the sleigh owners began eagerly firing back offers.

'Sixty kopeks.'

'Fifty.'

'Straight to the Eagle Market for just forty-five kopeks!'

This kind of bartering was the usual way of hiring transport in Russia; and it paid to bargain hard – and get a firm price. If not you might find yourself taking a very expensive trip; and I should add that these Russian sleigh drivers were not characters to be argued with after the event!

I hopped into the forty-five kopeks sleigh and off we went – at a full gallop.

Soon we were at the Eagle Market. Some of the birds were secured to perches, but many were in large baskets. Perch or basket, in proper market trader fashion, next to each eagle stood its owner, eagerly highlighting his bird's special qualities. What surprised me was that there wasn't a single Kirghiz or Kazakh amongst them. Most were Russians, but there were also a few Tartars and Bashkirs; there was even a Mordvin who spoke Finnish. All understood Russian.

As I gazed at the impressive selection of eagles the first thing to strike me was their size. They were noticeably bigger than Odin and although years later I would own Finnish eagles that were just as impressive, there and then, the impact they made almost had me launch into bartering. Indeed, if I hadn't been facing such a massive journey, that's exactly what I would have done. Instead, I swore to revisit the market on my return trip. It was of course a dream that would remain just that.

The following morning I boarded my train for the Kirghiz Steppe. The departure of a train in Russia – or Finland – was a far from straightforward affair. Ten minutes before the train was due to pull away, the stationmaster would appear on the platform and give a large wall-mounted brass bell a single ring. Eight minutes later he would come out again and ring the bell twice. When it was time for the train to depart, he would ring the bell three times, walk to the edge of the platform and unfurl a green flag or, at night, display a green lantern. Now another official would appear and blow a shrill whistle, this being replied to by the engine driver with a toot of the steam whistle. Finally, the locomotive would hiss and spit loudly, produce a cloud of steam and send a shower of sparks flying from its chimney as it slowly pulled away.

The cars themselves were tiny, each heated by a centrally positioned iron stove that the conductor fed with birch logs. Lighting was generally by gas, but sometimes a ceiling-suspended candle-lantern was the only thing available, which, despite the huge swan's neck of a candle it held, was useless for reading.

But as simple as things were, journeys were always enjoyable. It was a world moving at a different pace, the Finns and Russians being quick to quote the old saying: 'There's nothing more abundant than time.' Card games were started and harmonicas came out – and of course there was always enough vodka to ensure boredom was kept at bay.

My destination on this particular journey was a tiny settlement whose name now eludes me. As the train eventually came to a halt I disembarked, threw my bag over my shoulder and walked from the platform. I immediately spotted a group of four Kazakh horsemen who'd set up camp along the roadside. They'd been waiting for me.

We conversed in Russian and, greetings over, I was introduced to my transport, a little two-wheeled carriage designed to be pulled by a long pole that culminated in a crossbar. As I climbed aboard the contraption, two riders laid the crossbar across their saddles, and away we went – at full speed! Although the carriage had large wheels, the speed, coupled with the rough terrain, delivered a ride of pure agony. As soon as an opportunity arose I made my feelings about the hellish instrument of torture clear – something my companions found hilarious. Anyway, I refused to travel any further in the thing and demanded a horse, which I promptly got, the youngest member of the party jumping from the saddle to hand me the reins. He then sprang light as a cat onto the back of a spare horse, which had neither saddle nor bridle, and once again off we went.

It was afternoon by the time we reached our first camp. First out to welcome us was a pack of large and intimidating dogs, reassuringly followed by more benign inhabitants of the camp. One of my companions called out something in his native tongue and we were ushered into one of the yurts.

It was just as my uncle had described: a clever framework of wood over which was laid a skin of felt. Passing through a door-flap of sheep hides, I glanced around. In the centre was a fire, presumably for heating and cooking, the smoke from which escaped through a closable hole in the roof. And that was pretty much all the yurt contained; there wasn't a stick of furniture, a mix of grass mats and carpets providing the only seating.

The yurt was our accommodation that evening and after a huge meal of mutton – cooked over a fire of dried animal dung – we settled down on the mats and rugs, which, despite smelling of domestic stock, gave me a solid night's sleep.

The following morning we were on our way with fresh horses. On their ride out to meet me, my Kazakhs had changed horses at every stop and now, as they changed once again, the borrowed horses were being reunited with their rightful owners. That day, stopping at camps not too far apart, we changed horses four times, eventually spending the night at a group of five yurts – where the dreaded cart was also handed back to its owner.

Next day we saddled up again. Our final destination was just half a day's ride. Our mounts were now first class animals and it was clear that their owner, my host for the wolf hawking, was someone of wealth and high standing. By now I had also learned that two of my companions were his sons, while the oldest of the group was his wife's brother; he had his own camp some way out to the east.

My host's camp was very much like the others and populated by young and old – and of course more of those dogs. He himself was of senior years but appeared extremely fit and didn't carry an ounce of excess flesh. He was friendly but clearly a man of few words, my eagerly fired questions repeatedly fielded with a simple, 'You'll see.'

What immediately drew my attention were the two eagles perched between the yurts. Both were females and very impressive. Speaking in broken Russian, my host's sons informed me that one was a haggard* of unknown age: their father had purchased her from a Kirghiz falconer six years ago; she had cost two mares. The other bird was a three-year-old eyass** and had come from the Eagle Market. Both had taken wolves but the haggard was in a class of her own. Flown exclusively by their father, she was known all across the steppe as a top wolf-killer.

That evening it began to snow and a strong wind blew in. I knew that if this kept up there would be little chance of hawking. I lay on my rug listening to the howling wind and built a miserable picture of what the morning would bring: violent snowstorms, deep drifts and every able-bodied man desperately tending the flock. Hawking? The last thing on anyone's mind!

I've always been a light sleeper and so when two men entered the yurt at around midnight I was immediately awake. They were herders who had come to warm themselves and get something to eat. I quizzed them about the weather. Apparently the snow had stopped and the wind had died down – something confirmed by the walls of the yurt. In an attempt to tease me, they said that the weather was in fact far too good for hawking and it would have to be called off. I quickly let them know that I wasn't quite as wet behind the ears as they imagined and burst into an elaborate description of my hawking in Finland. Which impressed them not at all!

*A bird trapped after attaining mature plumage.

** A young bird taken from the nest.

The following morning I was woken by my host. When I asked if we were going hawking, a beaming smile introduced the very best news: not only was the weather perfect, wolf tracks had been found near the flock!

After a hearty breakfast, we – my host, his two sons and myself – saddled up and prepared to leave camp. Carefully, almost reverently, my host was handed the haggard. Her weight was borne by the horse, a wooden saddle-mounted support taking her owner's arm. She would be the only eagle flown, though it took firm words to relay this clearly to one son who was extremely eager to show off the younger eagle's talents. Going with us would be two dogs regularly used with the eagles. They were unlike any hunting breed I'd ever seen and I seriously doubted their value.

We were not far out of camp when we encountered wolf tracks. I jumped down to inspect them. 'These tracks were made sometime before midnight. The wolf could be over twenty kilometres from here by now.' My companions nodded in agreement. They too of course had noticed that the tracks were slightly blown over by snow, meaning they had been made after it had stopped snowing but before the wind had dropped. They knew too that a wolf often covers huge distances at night. Had the wolf killed a sheep, we might have been in luck: he would have found somewhere to sleep off his meal. As it was, our quest was hopeless.

Rather than follow the tracks any further, my host turned his horse towards a neighbouring camp, a whistle bringing the dogs straight from the trail.

By now it had clouded over, the dark sky bringing light rain. The snow began to thaw and from the hooves of the horse in front, great snowballs were periodically sent flying past my head.

Suddenly both dogs stopped. Wolf tracks! My host's sons and I dismounted: they were fresh, their owner apparently wandering without aim in a northerly direction. Was it the wolf from earlier? Had he perhaps indeed killed and was now looking for a resting place?

My host appeared optimistic: he would follow the tracks while we spread out on either side. The dogs, my respect for whom had grown considerably, went with my host.

After about twenty minutes we reached a big depression clogged with brush and dead reeds. It was surely the end of the hunt: if the wolf had entered this tangle we wouldn't even get a look at him, let alone a flight. My host however was not ready to admit defeat, a gesture of his hand immediately informing his sons of his plan. They called the dogs to us and, circling left, we rode to the far side of the depression: we were going to try and drive the wolf to their father.

Once in position we began our drive; I was in the middle. Being just three men strong, our line had massive gaps, the heavy cover hiding most of the ground between us. Even with the dogs, we were going to need a lot of luck. And it wasn't with us: the wolf was spotted briefly before escaping in the wrong direction.

We rode on to the neighbouring camp, where we were offered accommodation but given no positive news of wolves: they hadn't seen one for over two weeks. Undaunted, the next day we rode out and scoured the district for tracks. Nothing. But events were to take a surprise turn. During the afternoon, a young boy rode into camp excitedly informing us that a pack of wolves had taken several sheep from my host's son-in-law's flock. We were asked to return home immediately.

The news was music to my ears, something I tried to hide due to the unfortunate loss of the sheep. I looked across at my host and just for a second thought I caught him stifle his pleasure too.

Next day and back at our own camp, six of us with two eagles and two dogs were on our way to the son-in-law's base before dawn. I began to feel like a Kazakh, everything about this strange new world starting to take hold. The riding was fabulous. I'd grown up around horses and had even experimented with flying Odin from the saddle, but his kind of intensity was something totally new and I was hooked. From now on I'd be like a Kazakh and ride everywhere!

When we arrived at the son-in-law's camp the messenger's tale of woe was repeated. Six or seven wolves had been amongst the flock killing several sheep and also a calf and a filly. The evidence was there in front of us: wolf tracks everywhere and the snow littered red with sheep remains.

Leaving two of our party to help at camp, we divided our group: I stayed with my host and the haggard eagle; the two sons headed off with the younger bird. The dogs came with us.

There were tracks going in all directions but the dogs soon unravelled them to follow a single line heading into the steppe. The pace was brisk, my host occasionally needing to slow the dogs down. The wind was perfect: light and coming right at us.

I scanned the terrain to the right, my host, to the left; we both knew that our wolf would swing one way or the other to put himself behind us, thus getting our scent and probably even a look at us. It's a ploy also used by the fox and even the mountain hare.

We rode on and on, all the time following the dogs. I don't know how much time had passed but I had clearly allowed my attention to wander for suddenly the haggard sped past me close enough for her wingtips to strike my face! A panicked wolf was in full-flight and heading straight out across the steppe. My host came tearing by, his horse nearly colliding with mine as we took off in pursuit. The details of the capture were blurred by the chase, but we arrived to find the eagle in possession of her victim, which was still thrashing madly about. She had it by the head and shoulders, just as my own eagle dealt with foxes.

My host jumped from the saddle and drove a knife into the wolf's heart. Whether the eagle actually needed this help was, at that time, beyond my experience but years later I would see my own eagles kill our larger northern wolves totally unaided.

Despite the drama of it all, I found my excitement slightly tempered. The eagle was impressive and had flown well – and as my host dealt with the kill I made a point of expressing my admiration – but

something was missing. Was it that she wasn't mine and that I had been little more than a spectator? Perhaps it was the size of the quarry: this wolf wasn't a lot bigger than a strong Finnish fox. Then it struck me. The hounds! The hounds were missing. All my hawking at home revolved around my father's hounds, and the tension this created as I waited quietly on a run, listening to the pursuit's every turn and change in direction, not knowing when or where – or even if – the quarry would eventually show itself, was just as exciting as the flight itself; indeed, without this build up, the flight was a diamond in the darkness.

With the wolf thrown over my saddle, I handed my host his eagle and we made our way slowly back to his son-in-law's camp. On arriving we were informed that my host's sons had returned to camp and then set out again, taking an assistant and a dog. I was eager to try and catch them up, but my host insisted it was too late, dramatically adding that to spend a night out on the steppe was like visiting the camp of Genghis Khan: you might not make it back alive!

His sons returned late in the evening. They'd followed a set of wolf tracks all day but failed to get a glimpse of the animal itself. They were sure the wolf knew he was being followed. Maybe tomorrow would bring better luck.

Next morning the four of us rode out together. That night a lone wolf had been seen near the flock and we soon found his trail. Following the dogs at speed, we'd covered several versts* when one of my host's sons – carrying the young female eagle – almost rode over the wolf. It flushed so close to the horse the eagle was with it in seconds. Almost immediately wolves were flushing left and right – we'd ridden straight into their lair!

Now the haggard was slipped, and as she tackled her quarry I was able to follow the entire attack. First she grabbed the wolf in the back with just one foot. As the wolf then turned to bite, the other foot took hold of its head. The first foot then immediately moved to the chest, where the massive talons could deliver fatal injuries.

I was the first on the scene, my host soon arriving to dispatch the

*1 verst = approximately 1.1km or 0.7 miles

nearly dead wolf as before. It was a mature male. The son's eagle had taken a younger, much smaller wolf. We searched the area and discovered the remains of a filly the wolves had been feeding on.

I hawked with my Kazakh friends for another nine days, but we searched the entire area and found no further evidence of wolves. Our activities had obviously moved them on. And for me it was time to move on too: I was expected at Neratov's hunting lodge.

# 3
# North to Neratov

The journey that now lay ahead of me – a ride of several days across vast open country – would have caused me some concern had I been tackling it alone. Luckily I wasn't. It had been arranged for my Kazakh host's sons to accompany me; they knew the country, I had directions, and with Neratov known all across the Lower Urals, I was hoping to have little trouble finding his estate.

We changed horses three times during our first day, and probably covered the best part of a hundred versts. On we went, time being swallowed by the vastness of the country. It was now snowing every day and lying deeper the further we got into our journey. This forced us to slow our tempo and at times ride at walking pace. It was astonishing to watch my companions navigate through all this snow, going straight north as confident as birds heading for their breeding grounds. On several occasions I secretively compass-checked our route but couldn't fault their lead.

On the fourth day we arrived at a cabin on the shore of a small frozen lake. The entire valley was wooded – a welcome change after all that treeless country. An old Bashkir couple lived in the cabin: they fished the lake and had a few sheep, with generally a good enough crop of hay to keep them through the winter. They had only one worry: wolves.

'What about hunters?' I asked the old lady. 'Aren't there any wolf

hunters in the area?'

The woman laughed out loud. 'That's the problem. We have too many wolf hunters. But do you think they shoot wolves? No. Here they entice more of them to come in from other areas. Yes, that's what they are doing, pampering wolves so the rich and mighty can chase them with their borzois.'

'And who finances all of this?' I inquired.

'That I don't know, and I don't want to know either. In fact I've probably said too much already. Ask at the village. Maybe someone there will talk to you about it. We've got a peaceful life here and want it to stay that way.' Her husband, who appeared to be deaf but apparently understood everything she said, nodded in agreement.

We drank tea with them then rode on. A few hours later we arrived at a valley with a small stream running through it, and now for the first time we changed direction and rode west, following the stream. Soon we came to a Cossack village. It was so well tucked away in the trees that we had ridden right into it before registering it was there. At once the headman was called. As expected he demanded to see our papers. I showed him mine and explained that the two Kazakhs were accompanying me. I was a little concerned that this might cause a problem, but after a glance at my pass – which I don't think he could actually read – we were invited to tea and kringles. The latter were always offered in Russia and eastern Finland and produced in vast quantities. They were tasty but required the strongest of teeth!

After we had finished our tea, I inquired if our host knew of Neratov. 'Of course! Everyone knows Neratov. The latest news is that he has some special stones stuck in the snow and sets them on fire. The spectacle starts about forty versts from his hunting lodge and lights up the road like the Nevsky Prospect in St. Petersburg. The great winter wolf hunt starts in a few days and important guests are arriving every day, big landowners and noblemen from the Urals and the Don – even top names from St. Petersburg and Moscow. The flaming stones greet them as they arrive.'

'And how far is it to Neratov's hunting lodge?' I asked.

He smiled, or at least seemed to, an enormous beard that hung down to his belly hid most of his face. 'Oh, about thirty versts, I would say. The road down by the stream goes past it. Do you have a message or something for him?'

'No, I'm invited to the wolf hunt.'

Now the beard couldn't hide the expression beneath it. 'Of course you are Your Royal Highness! I suppose you're related to the German Kaiser or the King of Sweden! Go tell your tall tales to the village children, I've no time for such nonsense.' And he grabbed me by the collar and pushed me away.

My Kazakh companions had been silent but now stepped in. 'Show some respect! A king's son he may not be but his uncle is head of the Nobel Company in Baku and we have been sent to accompany him to Neratov's hunting lodge.'

Once again I handed him my papers. 'It's all here, read it for yourself.' As before he glanced quickly at them, not even taking them from my hand. But now his tone changed.

'Your Grace must know that the Tsar doesn't like strangers riding about the steppe. In fact I have orders to detain anyone considered suspicious. Now, ride in peace, and if Your Grace wishes I can provide a man who knows the way.'

We were actually more in need of fresh horses: it was only thirty versts and could be accomplished that very day with fresh mounts. I thought I'd try my luck. 'Thank you for your kind offer. Could you also possibly supply three horses? Your man and my two companions will return them tomorrow.' It didn't take him long to answer and his agreement was delivered with clear relief: any unpleasantness caused a guest of Neratov's could lead to serious trouble, especially so close to his lodge.

It was pitch black by the time we joined the final approach to the lodge. Three hundred metres from the door we brought the horses to a stop. Left and right of the road, flames were shooting out of the snow and where the snow was too deep to allow this, there was a deep glow of beautiful red. It may not have been a display stretching forty versts like the Cossack had claimed but it was still most impressive. My companions just stared in wonderment, something I had done some five years earlier when the first carbide lamps reached Finland.

We proceeded along the drive, snow-laden trees casting their shadows in the moonlight, stars flickering brightly, and before us the magnificent hunting lodge, its windows lit warm and inviting with a multitude of different colours. It was a magical scene.

As we rode through the gates, dogs began to bark and a group of men in snow-white fur coats came running out. We must have looked anything but important guests and caused some surprise when we rode straight to the main entrance. I jumped off my horse and a tall, stately man came over. It was Neratov's huntmaster, Gerasimov. I gave him my name and explained that the Kazakhs and the Cossack had assisted me and would be leaving in the morning. 'Your Grace is expected,' he said politely. 'We will tend to the men and horses.' And with that, he heaved open the huge front door. 'Please enter.'

Inside I was met by Lisizin. It was a warm welcome. He and my father had been friends for years. Indeed, in 1888 both had visited America to study the latest developments in the steel industry. They brought back a small tray that was probably the first aluminium item ever seen in Finland. It was a marvel, everyone astounded by its lightness. During their trip they also visited Niagara Falls, and my father had a photo showing them both standing on the stony shore below the falls. How strange that a lifetime later I would buy a retirement farm only a short distance from where the photo was taken.

A servant brought my saddlebags and I asked Lisizin where I could change. But he immediately grabbed my arm and led me to the dining room where a huge table was set. There were plates of cheeses from every corner of the globe, countless types and cuts of meat, caviar, pickled herrings, baskets full of bread and of course – lots of vodka.

'I bet you could use some nourishment after a long day's ride?' he suggested. 'Neratov and most of his guests are sleeping off a session of heavy celebrating, so I'm playing stand-in host. Come on, tuck in!' I didn't need much encouragement and loaded a plate with meat, cheese and caviar and settled down to enjoy my meal. Lisizin swiftly halted me. 'You can't eat like a pig around here!' I knew the old Russian joke and poured myself a glass of vodka: pigs don't drink alcohol with their food. Lisizin stayed and kept me company, a bottle of vodka making sure no piggish ways crept in!

I glanced into the hall and could see an assortment of snoring bodies, some were in chairs, some on couches and some even on the floor. Lisizin laughed. 'Those are the ones who didn't make it as far as their rooms.' They'd clearly had a lively evening, or more accurately, morning. I hadn't expected anything else. The Russian aristocracy – indeed all in high social standing – had turned their lives upside down: day was now night, night, day. The women never rose before six in the evening. If an officer's wife, she would be bathed by his servant, and then with his help spend until eight or nine making herself beautiful. Around eleven o'clock she would accompany her husband to restaurants, casinos and other places of amusement to eat, drink and dance through the night. Around six in the morning she would return home to sleep. When the men actually slept was always a mystery to me – probably at the barracks or in their offices. They were such a degenerate band it's a wonder the revolution didn't arrive sooner.

Lisizin told me that most of the hunting staff were scheduled to ride out before daybreak to find and encircle some wolves. The first drive would be at noon. I asked him if he thought Neratov would object to me riding along. He didn't think so and rang for a servant. 'Tell the Master of the Hunt that this gentleman wishes to ride out with him in the morning and that he should be awakened in time.' With that, I went to find my room; I was desperate for sleep and knew I wouldn't get any once the other guests woke up.

Early next morning Gerasimov and I crept out of a rear door so as to avoid the guests, who were now once again in full swing. He was friendly but I noticed a slight uneasiness about him and he didn't seem that comfortable with me. Perhaps it was my age: it was unheard of for a sixteen year old to be invited on a wolf hunt; was he being reserved due to some special status he thought I possessed?

We made our way to the stables where about forty riders were waiting. We mounted up and with the stars gleaming brightly, left the estate. I fell in alongside Gerasimov and we began to chat, and if there had been any coolness on his part it soon faded away as our shared love of the chase began to work its magic.

Soon we were in forest-steppe country, undulating ground containing a mix of steppe, forest and brush as far as the eye could see. With the red of the breaking day rising over this snow-covered wilderness the picture was one of incredible beauty.

Gerasimov gave the order to spread out, and as the command was passed down the line all unnecessary noise was forbidden. As we moved forwards, each man examined the ground carefully, every track meticulously checked. Before long we saw the silhouettes of six Kazakh riders coming towards us. They rode straight to Gerasimov. They had encircled a pack of wolves in a small wood and had also found the tracks of other wolves further east; several of their group were attempting to encircle these as well. Gerasimov told me that Neratov paid these Kazakhs so well for each wolf they found they could live comfortably from the proceeds. He suspected they were even helping the wolves to breed, for nowhere else were they so common. It was in fact known that long before Christmas old horses were being slaughtered in various places to attract them. The old lady at the lake had been right.

Gerasimov sent word back to the lodge that the guests, remaining hunt staff and the hound and borzoi handlers should join us.

There wasn't much for us to do now except wait. One of the Kazakhs informed us of a small wood that lay in the direction of the surrounded wolf pack: it might be a suitable spot to arrange a makeshift camp. His suggestion met with approval and we were soon settled in front of three roaring fires. Hunting tales began to flow. Gerasimov told of a Mordvin who'd taught a bear to dance and travelled from village to village entertaining the crowds. However, as time passed the bear became more and more unmanageable, which signalled an end to the enterprise. Stuck with a bear he no longer wanted, when late autumn arrived he took it into the forest, built it a den and chained it down. When the bear went into hibernation, he removed the chain and set about advertising the chance to shoot a bear, eventually selling the 'hunt' to some gullible young fool. When this chap and two of his friends arrived for their big day, the Mordvin, also with a companion, took them to the den and began poking deep into the snow to wake the bear, which had barely got its eyes open before the Mordvin began screaming, 'Shoot! Shoot!' Which the hunters did and off home they went with their prize.

Later the Mordvin's companion asked him why he'd been in such a hurry to have the bear shot. Was he frightened it might run away? 'Run away. Not at all. But if I'd left him to wake properly he might have started to dance!'

Gerasimov winked at one of the Kazakhs. 'Maybe one day we'll see a wolf do a dance before hightailing it!'

'My father,' I said, 'once arranged a bear hunt for two wealthy industrialists from France. The hunt was to take place north of his mining operation in an area of state-owned forest. My job was to act as sleigh driver and interpreter; one of them spoke fluent German. I was also to take a cockerel, something my father had promised the head forester who was a longstanding friend. A fox had killed his own and his hens had stopped laying.

' "What's the cockerel for?" asked the German speaker. And before my father, who was standing on the steps behind us, had a chance to comment, I said, "To wake us early enough for the hunt. I understand that in France you have clocks that can be set to wake you up, but in Finland we have no such devices."

'My father played along, "Make sure you put the cockerel near the heater at night or he won't wake up early enough."

'With the journey being long, we had to stay overnight at a farmhouse and I made a big fuss of bringing the cockerel in and placing it close to the stove, from where, an hour before daybreak, it did its duty and began to crow.

'On arriving at the forester's, I quickly let him in on the joke and his alarm clock was swiftly hidden away. The cockerel came in for the night and was placed close to the stove.

'After the Frenchmen had shot their bear we returned home. I of course left the cockerel, explaining that the forester was in great need of it. Three months later my father received a newspaper clipping describing the hunt in great detail; it also explained how in Finland there were no alarm clocks and that travellers wishing to rise early had to take a cockerel everywhere with them. A week later a parcel arrived. It contained a thank you note and an alarm clock!'

With the mood as warm as our campfires, the tales continued until the hunt staff and houndsmen appeared in the distance. The borzois looked magnificent, moving over the terrain with effortless ease. I was mesmerized by their height and noble appearance – and also by the length of the slender head and jaws. If ever there was a dog that looked a match for a full-grown wolf, this was it.

With the guests being slowly brought up, the rest of us advanced in the direction of the surrounded wolves.

We could see the wood from some way off and now those in charge of the hounds dismounted. They would wait for the guests; to take the hounds any closer was to risk them sensing the wolves, becoming excited and causing them to break out prematurely.

The borzoi handlers split into groups, ready to position themselves around the wood. I accompanied them, joining an elderly man and two of the most attractive borzois in the group. Gerasimov stayed with the hounds.

My companion and I halted some six hundred metres north of the wood. It was a position chosen in relation to possible escape routes: this wood was one of several such 'islands' and according to the Kazakhs there was a reed valley to the east that offered still better sanctuary.

Time crawled; my excited mind raced. Would the wolves hold steady in the wood until the guests arrived? And if they didn't, would we – the borzoi handlers – notice their exit? We were a good verst apart and the terrain was by no means fully visible: there were numerous little hills and valleys; a wolf – an entire pack – might manage to slink away undetected. Were they still there at all? We would only know once the hounds were released.

The air was still and crystal clear. Complete silence. Suddenly my companion pointed north. Out on the steppe I could see eight troikas storming through the snow, accompanied by Kazakh riders. It was an astonishing scene. The Kazakhs soon pulled up and the troikas divided into two groups, one going to the left of the wood, the other to the right.

As the cavalcade rushed past I could see that most of the troikas contained just one guest. It was as I'd expected: only a quarter of the guests had managed to rise in time for the hunt. Not even Neratov had made it, being replaced by Lisizin.

The hound handlers now set off for the wood, while those with borzois moved closer to make the ring tighter. About a hundred metres from the wood, my companion and I stopped. It was a good position: we had a backdrop of cover to make us less obvious to any wolf coming out of the wood and also had an excellent view of the terrain. I was now entrusted with one of the borzois. We were ready.

Once again my mind went into overdrive. Would the wolf pack come in our direction, or favour someone else? Would the pack in fact stay together at all, or break up to have individual animals flushing from various spots? Who could say, but the hounds were now at work, the dice thrown.

Suddenly a hound gave tongue. It was barely audible, yet it was as if a gun had gone off right beside me. I glanced at my companion and was astonished by his composure: he might have been waiting for a hare rather than a wolf! He noticed me staring and just smiled. Perhaps he remembered his own first wolf hunt.

The hounds could now be heard in all directions. 'The pack has broken up,' he whispered. Then, appearing as if by magic, at the edge of the wood, a wolf. A few agonising seconds passed, the wolf just standing there gazing in our direction. Could he see us? More likely he just didn't trust the open ground. He certainly couldn't have caught our scent, the wind was wrong for that. Then as quickly as he'd appeared, he vanished. I looked at my companion, whose eyes screamed back 'Don't move!' Suddenly the wolf was back. With no hound on his trail he was in no hurry to commit himself. I was shaking with excitement.

Throughout all of this our borzois had remained totally calm. Not having our height, they had been unable to see the wolf and their noses were clearly not good enough to pick up his scent

About half a kilometre to my right I saw a rider and troika racing across the steppe. A wolf must have broken out. Damn it, I thought, they'll scare our wolf back into the trees. But they didn't. He remained motionless and they disappeared over a rise.

Then suddenly his hand was forced: two hounds appeared behind him and he flew towards us. With the hounds trailing in his wake, he passed us at something like seventy metres. We immediately slipped the borzois. In the same instant my companion swung himself into the saddle and was away. I wasn't as quick, but my horse was faster and I had soon taken the lead.

The wolf was fast – and also cunning, using every bush and hollow to lose his pursuers. I swung left in an attempt to cut him off, and the borzois, who'd momentarily lost sight of him, followed. Soon they got sight of him again and the chase was back on. My companion had been left some way back.

The wolf was now a couple of hundred metres ahead of me with the borzois in close pursuit. This was the moment of truth. The bitch borzoi made an attempt to seize the wolf by the throat. Her quarry retaliated by attempting to bite, but he missed his mark and she had him. I arrived a few seconds later to find both borzois in possession of

an already dead wolf. It was a young animal that had not yet gained its full strength. My companion soon arrived and a few minutes later so did the hounds, still hot on the wolf's trail.

My companion was in a hurry. He leashed the borzois, threw the wolf across his saddle and mounted without tying the carcass down. 'Come on! We have to get back to our post, it's not covered.' We set off, the hounds following.

At length we were back in position and waiting in silence. Indeed, all around was silent: not a murmur from hounds or hunters. The two hounds were desperate to return to the wood, so my companion threw down the dead wolf. While they sniffed around it I leashed them up.

Soon a messenger rode over. Apparently the wood was now empty and we should ride to its eastern side where everyone was gathering: some of the Kazakhs had managed to encircle a single wolf some way off and it was hoped that this might provide another chance for the borzois.

At the meeting place we found five troikas and a strong team of houndsmen and Kazakhs. Three troikas had gone back to the lodge.

Their occupants were perhaps still feeling the effects of their partying and, having seen enough sport – an old female wolf and two youngsters had been caught – were ready to retire.

It seemed about time I introduced myself to the other guests, who must have been wondering who this young fellow was galloping about the steppe. Lisizin broke the ice, announcing me loud and clear. Various greetings came back and the formality was over with.

It was now late and we made haste, troikas, riders, hounds and borzois forming a scattered procession – which very soon got a more orderly shape as an old and respected Cossack pulled us into a column that would have been the pride of any parade ground.

Before long we arrived at the encircled wolf. To each troika was detailed a brace of borzois and a handler. I got the same team as before, staying with my horse rather than switching to one of the troikas. The remaining borzois were kept back. The troikas were sent to surround the narrow reed-thick valley that supposedly held the wolf and twenty minutes later the houndsmen rode down and released their hounds.

The sun was now setting and a light fog began to rise from the valley. The afternoon had become noticeably colder. The hounds were totally silent and I wondered if the wolf hadn't perhaps escaped.

Suddenly we heard the hounds. They were at a massive distance, their voices only periodically audible. 'Well,' said my companion, 'the wolf has left the valley. For us the hunt is over.' About fifteen minutes later a rider appeared through the fading light: Lisizin's borzois had killed the wolf.

We mounted up and turned for home. The stars shone brightly in the ink blue sky and in front of us the troikas moved phantom-like through the snowy landscape, their sleigh bells, removed during the hunt, now ringing out our homeward journey. Slowly the troop of riders behind us began to sing. It was an old song that mingled with the bells in the cold night air to create an unforgettable symphony of the steppe. My happiness was total.

As we rode on my mind moved to our destination and what it held. From my earliest childhood I had been a loner, shy amongst strangers and at my happiest out in the forests with my brother and the hounds. Now I was faced with all Neratov's guests, those who had remained behind probably still drunk, those returning with us, planning to quickly join them.

We arrived back at the lodge to find a military band playing in the courtyard. Oh, how I longed to just disappear into the servants' hall along with the staff. But there was no avoiding it. I slipped in behind Lisizin and went straight to Neratov, who was greeting the returning guests.

'There you are!' he called out as soon as he saw me. 'The new Master of the Hunt!' I thanked him enthusiastically for the wonderful day's hunting, and Lisizin, who appeared to be in exceptionally good humour – perhaps due to his success against the final wolf – commented that I'd nearly died of excitement!

Neratov ushered us in to the dining hall, where the celebrations were already in full swing. Seeing that none of those who had been on the hunt were bothering to change, I too kept my riding clothes on.

From childhood Russian Sterlett caviar had been one of my favourite foods, and now, staring at a huge mound of it, I skipped everything else and loaded my plate, adding just French bread and butter. I then eased in beside Lisizin at a small table, where, without needing to be encouraged, I also sampled some of the six varieties of vodka on offer. The meal continued with soup. Two types were available: Borsch, made with beetroot, and Seljanka, an excellent fish soup. Despite its fabulous reputation, I had never cared for Borsch and so opted for the Seljanka. This was followed by roast bear, something I was familiar with and also didn't much care for, or venison. I should add that this meal was only intended as a homecoming appetiser, dinner itself would be served at eleven that evening.

Helped along by the vodka, my shyness soon evaporated and I found myself involved in lively conversations at all points of the table. Neratov was keen to hear more of my uncle in Baku. He'd heard of his toughness and no-nonsense attitude, qualities he admired. And tough my uncle certainly was. He inhabited a world where death might be only a dark alley away; indeed two attempts had already been made on his life, one of these earning him the title Bullet Proof, which added still more weight to his already fearsome reputation.

Drinking and exchanging hunting tales – which of course became more exaggerated by the hour – time passed swiftly and before long we were informed that dinner was about to be served. Throughout this mammoth feast I sat next to an elderly gentleman called Nikolai Nikoaijevitz, a colonel who'd taken part in the Russian-Turkish war. When I commented on how fine the meal had been, he responded, 'Not bad, but the younger generation don't have any idea how to celebrate properly. In my youth it was different. I recall how the musicians, having played all night, would be chased up in to trees and brought down with rifles. Those were the days!'

After another glass of cognac he suddenly stood up and yelled, 'Where are the hunting staff? Out on the steppe their Cossack songs made my heart ache. Bring them in: we demand a song!'

His suggestion was well received and a loud chant echoed through the hall, 'Bring them in, bring them in!' Whether this suited Neratov or not was hard to say. His narrow face with its hard blue eyes gave little away. He was a watcher, noting all but parting with nothing. Even under the influence of alcohol he was the same, his gaze like a secret scope peering over the edge of a battle trench. And it was a gaze that could fix you with a shudder, should the crosshairs fall on you.

Our entertainers – apparently dragged from bed – appeared in less than ten minutes. My new friend, Colonel Nikoaijevitz, grabbed a champagne cooler, emptied it into another and proceeded to add vodka, cognac and wine. He then climbed onto the table and yelled, 'Here Cossacks! Drink to the honour of General Gourko, and to the memory of Plavna, Nikopol, Kars, Tyronow and Tashkissenei!'

They didn't need asking twice and the colonel's lethal cocktail was soon being passed around. With a deep voice the colonel began one of the Cossack songs we had enjoyed on our return ride from the hunt. The lead singer, who had a beautiful tenor voice, joined in and soon everyone was involved. It couldn't of course capture the atmosphere we'd had out on the steppe, but it was pretty impressive. The mood rose by the minute, still more alcohol having Colonel Nikoaijevitz bursting into a solo performance. It was all getting a bit wild. I looked for Neratov but he'd disappeared.

Lisizin came over. 'Come on, let's get some sleep.'

'Do you think we'll be hunting tomorrow?'

'Certainly.'

'With these hunt staff!'

'Trust me. They'll be in the saddle even if they're unable to walk.'

Suddenly all hell broke loose. The hunt staff had grabbed the colonel and begun to toss him high into the air accompanied by wild calls. Lisizin grabbed my arm and pulled me away. Maybe he was afraid the same honour would soon befall him. We left, leaving poor Nikoaijevitz being flung about like a helpless rag doll.

I wasn't as sure about the morning's hunt as Lisizin. Nevertheless, sleep came quickly and it seemed I'd hardly closed my eyes when I was being woken again. It was Gerasimov.

'We're leaving in half an hour.' I dressed quickly and followed him. The whole house seemed dead.

As previously we left by a rear exit, met the other men, mounted up and took the same route as the day before. We stopped at the site of our makeshift camp and were met by a Kazakh. Eighteen of his comrades were trying to encircle a group of wolves. While they did this there was nothing to do but wait, so we built some fires and settled down.

Before the first breeze of morning had risen, two Kazakhs rode in to camp. Two packs containing approximately thirteen wolves had been encircled: to prevent them breaking out flag lines would be needed. Gerasimov ordered twenty men back to the lodge to fetch these and inform the hound and borzois handlers.

To pass the time I helped the remaining men gather firewood. Gerasimov sat on a log without speaking. In passing, I enquired at what time the guests had finally retired. Without looking up he mumbled that he had no idea and turned to poke the fire. His mood puzzled me; indeed, everyone seemed a little subdued. Was it just the after effects of the drinking?

Finally the flag lines arrived and two Kazakhs jumped onto their horses to guide the sleigh to the required spot. As I was tired of waiting around I rode with them, quickly followed by a member of staff who had been assigned to stay with me.

The wolves were in a large wood stretching southwards. We rode around it in a large arc, until the Kazakhs finally halted and dismounted. One of them threw a frame-supported reel on his back, onto which the flag line had been wound. As he walked, the line unwound from the reel and his companion hung it on bits of brush so that its little cloth flags, tied at about three quarter of a metre intervals, were suspended just above the snow, flapping in the wind. Two more Kazakhs with a second reel followed, hanging their line a little higher. In essence they were creating a brightly coloured fence through which no wolf would pass.

I watched for a while then returned to the edge of the wood where my companion was waiting. The sleigh had disappeared. The two of us now rode to the north end of the wood to await the hounds and borzois. They arrived about half an hour later. Now the north end of the wood was quickly surrounded. Neratov's guests were expected at any minute

and the men had barely taken their positions before the first troikas roared into sight.

Each troika was assigned a brace of borzois and a handler. The houndsmen then circled around the wood and broke into it near the start of the flag line.

Accompanied by the handler and borzois from the day before, I was positioned to the north, the position next to me being occupied by Neratov. There was a better turn out than the previous day – most of the troikas containing two guests – but I did notice that Colonel Nikoaijevitz was nowhere to be seen.

Before long some of the hounds gave tongue, and a few minutes later four wolves broke from the wood and ran for Neratov's post. His assistant waited for them to pass then slipped his borzois.

The pursuit went straight west. As the two borzois closed on one of the wolves, the three others turned south and appeared to be heading back to the wood. In an effort to prevent them reaching it, my companion and I unleashed our borzois and rode for all we were worth to try and cut them off. We were about four hundred metres from the wolves when our borzois spotted them, and now for the first time I realised how swift these dogs were: they left us as if we were walking!

The gap between pursued and pursuers began to shrink. The excitement was at fever pitch: the wood was in sight; would the wolves make it? Then it happened. One minute I was racing over the ground, the

next flying through the air. My horse had stumbled. I landed several metres away and the light covering of soft snow offered no cushion at all from the frozen ground beneath. The impact blew the air out of my lungs, leaving me gasping for breath at the end of a series of violent rolls. At which point I must have passed out. The next thing I recall is my borzoi handler standing over me. 'What happened to the wolves?' I asked.

'We caught one, an old male.'

He helped me to my feet and I made a few staggering steps towards my horse. I was as dizzy as a drunk.

'Can I help you into the saddle?'

'Just a minute. Let me try it on my own first.'

I grabbled hold of the mane, stuck my boot into the stirrup and swung myself up.

There I sat, and felt like death.

At that moment a troika pulled up. It was Neratov. 'I think you should perhaps ride with me in the troika. I have to return to the lodge anyway.'

I thanked him but said I would rather stay and continue the hunt. He signalled his driver and they pulled away. His departure puzzled me: he was leaving his guests and the hunt? I quizzed my companion. He knew nothing other than a messenger had come out from the lodge and whatever the note contained it was obviously important enough to prompt Neratov's immediate return.

We rode back to our position, but my chest was now becoming more and more painful; the slightest pressure was agony. Having had broken ribs several times before, it was something I was familiar with. Previously however the damage had been to one side only. Now I was sure I had breaks on both sides. I didn't say anything but was relieved when a rider arrived informing us that the woods were clear and we were to head home. We made our way to the assembly point where we found most of the guests already waiting. Only two troikas were missing. By this time I was in real pain, my left shoulder also very uncomfortable.

Lisizin came over to ask how I was: news of my accident had travelled as fast as a borzoi. I said I was okay and mentioned having seen Neratov before he left for the lodge. At this he became surprisingly attentive and was eager to know if he had said anything. I was now convinced something serious had happened.

The troikas led the way home, their bells ringing out again as we went. But this time there was no singing or joyful banter, just silence. Gerasimov wheeled round furiously in his saddle, 'Have you all gone deaf and dumb! Give us a song!' A lone voice began and others fell in with him. But it was clearly forced and not at all to Gerasimov's liking. 'May the devil fill your throats with pig shit! You may as well be quiet if that's the best you can do! I'm just about ready to throttle the lot of you, except the one I'll spare to bury the rest!' There was deadly silence.

Back at the lodge Neratov was waiting for us. He invited us all into the great hall and signalled that the doors be closed. 'Gentlemen,' he said, 'our old friend and hunting companion Nikolai Nikoaijevitz is dead. He suffered a heart attack. I am told he was discovered in bed having been seen to his quarters quite well after the festivities.' He looked around the room. 'I have accepted this as a true account of what happened and am assuming, my friends, you agree with my decision. If anyone has anything to say, now is the time.' No one spoke.

'Good!' said Neratov. 'That's the last we will say of this unhappy occurrence. Tomorrow the hunt continues.' At which he rang a bell, and servants, who must have been waiting behind the door, appeared with trays of champagne. Glasses were raised. 'To the memory of our friend Nikolai Nikoaijevitz!' The colonel was then struck from the guest list.

From experience I knew that instead of easing, broken ribs actually became more painful for the first week to ten days, and with my shoulder also to consider, I went to see Lisizin. He agreed: further hunting was out of the question. He was travelling to St. Petersburg in the morning and I could join him. After explaining to Neratov and impressing on him how wonderful I had found it all I went over to the servants' quarters to bid farewell to Gerasimov. I found him with a glass of vodka in front of him, a glass soon joined by another as he invited me to sit. We talked of the hunting, my ribs and of poor Nikolai Nikoaijevitz. Finally, with a firm and true promise that I would always be welcome, I went to bed.

Next morning the stars were sparkling as I came out of the lodge. The snow protested my every step across the courtyard and from the waiting troika came the ring of sleigh bells every time the horses shook themselves. The driver covered us up to our breasts with a huge blanket made of fox skins, then swung onto the driver's seat, grabbing the reins. The sleigh's runners squealed loudly as the horses pulled away, tree trunks snapped and crackled in the cold and on the not too distant lake the ice could be heard moaning. I looked back. I would never forget this place.

Years later I discovered that Nikolai Nikoaijevitz had not died of a heart attack but had been killed during the mad flinging session. His head had struck an item of furniture.

# 4
# Hagenbeck's Lynx

In my youth, the lynx was a highly prized quarry, and doubly valuable if secured without shotgun damage to its pelt. Still more profitable was to take the animal alive: Hagenbeck's Zoo in Hamburg had an agent in Sortavala who was always ready to pay good money for a live lynx. The way to secure such an animal was to run it down on skis, the targeted lynx being simply pursued to exhaustion. The founder of this ski hunting is thought to be Heikki Auvonen who discovered that a lynx was unable to run at full speed for more than half an hour before becoming exhausted; at a slower pace it could keep going for three or four days, and even then it might be victorious over its pursuer.

Once caught, the quarry had to be handled with great skill. The lynx is a powerhouse of muscle and sinew – a leggy cat the size of a small doberman with absolutely lethal feet. When tackled it becomes a spitting, hissing fireball of action and an opponent underestimated at great cost. The safest way to deal with it was to press it into the snow with the skis and give it an old leather glove attached to a ski stick to bite on. Only then was an attempt made to secure it.

I was involved in a lynx capture early on in my hunting career, though it was no ski chase, coming more under the heading, 'unconventional'. It was in the autumn of 1905.

'So, do those droopy-eared mutts of yours eat dog flesh?' asked my

hunting companion as he ceased poking the campfire and pointed his stick at the two hounds sleeping beside me. This Karelian wilderness man sorted dogs into just two types: those with pointed ears, like the spitz, and those with what he termed lid-ears, like my hounds – which he didn't rate at all.

'Dog flesh?' I said with surprise. 'I've never tried them on it.'

'Well, there you are,' he said as he moved the kettle with his left hand. His right hand had been missing since last winter. A bear had bitten it off. Not while hunting, though he was a well-known bear hunter. No, it was an accident of quite a different nature. Three years earlier he'd taken a young cub from a female he'd shot, hoping he'd be able to sell it as a pet. However, he couldn't find a buyer and so kept it. As it got bigger, the two of them practised 'bear wrestling' but the Karelian always had to let the bear win or it would become furious. Well, the previous year he'd been at a market trying to sell the bear by demonstrating its wrestling abilities. Unfortunately, during one of these demonstrations he didn't let the bear win quickly enough and it bit off his hand.

He continued, 'I can see that you don't know much about bear and lynx dogs for it's a clear waste of time to try and hunt any carnivore with a dog that won't eat the meat of its own kind. We give our bear-hunting spitz a chunk of dog meat as soon as they have their teeth. If they don't eat it, they are not continued with. Such a dog will never hunt lynx or bear.'

'Well, for most of my hunting I don't need a dog that fearlessly attacks. In fact some of my hounds won't even kill a hare if they catch it – which sometimes happens when the snow is deep. But that doesn't mean they are useless as hare dogs. After all, we're not dragging these guns along as ballast!'

'Your kind are a strange sort,' he continued undaunted, 'always reaching for a gun when trapping is so much easier and more profitable. If I hadn't known you for so long I wouldn't have come on this idiot's errand. Just consider. It's now the end of October. In two months the snow will be over a metre deep and we could chase any lynx we find down on skis. This would give us a pelt worth six times the money and be less work. Doesn't that make more sense?'

'You call that less work? Anyway, it looks like your lynx hunting days are over. Just be careful you don't feed your other hand to the bear and end up in the poorhouse!'

Now he just grinned. 'He won't be doing me or anyone else any harm now. He's as tame as a bride after the honeymoon and as harmless as the eunuch from Valamo.* I got young Vornanen to help me and we castrated him!'

'How did you ever manage that?' I said in surprise.

'We supplied him with so much booze he fell asleep, and afterwards he had such a hangover he didn't even notice.'

'What a frightful tale and one we will leave there. It'll be daylight in half an hour. Let's get ready.'

The morning was icy cold and the thought of leaving the still-warm fire we had spent the night by, was very unappealing. For over two weeks now the closed-hoof rather than splayed tracks of moose had crossed the swamps and it seemed to get colder by the day. We were in the Karelian wilderness, about one hundred kilometres north of Lake Ladoga. We had been underway for several days. In the endless taiga hares were proving few and difficult for the hounds to work. The much-wanted snow had stayed away and the frozen poor-scent ground was giving the hounds trouble following their quarry's circling and long-leap escape manoeuvres. It was trouble we didn't need: our real goal was the lynx, a much simpler animal for the hounds under these conditions. However, so far we'd only managed to put up a fox and six hares – which we'd shot and fed to the hounds. Our own diet had consisted of nothing but hazel grouse, which were plentiful. Capercaillie and black grouse had also been an option but we hadn't wanted to overload ourselves. We had enough to drag along as it was: guns, ammunition, blankets, butter and salt, a kettle, and of course an axe, without which you never went into the wilderness.

As we had finished eating, I decided to give the hounds the leftovers. My friend protested, insisting that if fed they would lose their

* A monastery in Lake Ladoga.

ability to follow a trail and be useless for the rest of the day. It was a 'no food before work rule' adhered to by many of the older houndsmen. I ignored him and threw them the grouse bones.

When the last of the bones had disappeared I unleashed the dogs and we set off. The frozen moss crunched under our heavy boots and the occasional screeching of jays was joined by the odd hazel grouse call; but from the hounds there wasn't a sound. Indeed, the early part of the day unfolded pretty uneventfully.

Then we put up a fox. This however immediately went to ground, bringing the Karelian and myself to loggerheads. I wanted to move on; he wanted to set a trap by the earth and wait, arguing that in two days at the most we'd have our prize, sporting an undamaged pelt worth a good price. Not bad work, as he put it, for two sleeping men. In fact, only a dumb Swede, which I was in his books, wouldn't grasp the logic. We moved on anyway.

It was almost noon and we'd only seen the hounds a couple of times, though they were following well. In deep forest this is quite normal: the wide searches limit visual contact. I dropped my rucksack and suggested a break, something my friend had probably been waiting for.

I'd only just sat down when the bitch hound suddenly gave tongue and the male joined her. A hare, I thought to myself and began to look for a likely looking run. My friend, clearly showing his lack of interest in the whole business, followed reluctantly – so reluctantly in fact that we were soon completely separated.

The hunt was in full flight and went straight away from me and almost out of hearing range. Then there was a turn as hounds and quarry came back, passing just beyond my field of vision. I now wondered if it really was a hare and hurried to where the pursuit had passed. The hounds were now silent: it had to be a fox. I wanted to let the Karelian know but couldn't bellow the news through the forest.

Still no sound from the hounds. I thought I heard them briefly in the far distance but then all was quiet again. Had they lost the trail? Or had the fox gone to ground? All I could do was wait.

Then suddenly the hunt was on again, but far, far away. Well, this was certainly no hare. A hare would never make such a long run, not even in the coldest winter weather. Could it be a lynx?

The hunt drew closer and was coming straight at me. I readied myself. When the hounds came within sight, at about two hundred metres, I assumed their quarry had somehow passed me. Disappointed, I watched as the hounds disappear again, wondering where they would show up next.

The pursuit now turned sharp right, going away from me. Had the fox or lynx caught my scent? This would have been easy: the wind was totally wrong and blowing every detail to whatever creature was out there. Damn it!

I'd hardly finished cursing when there in front of me stood a lynx. It was just there as if it had grown from the forest floor. He was no more than twenty steps away and looking over his back towards the hounds with his short stubby tail standing straight up. Slowly, very slowly I raised the gun, but the lynx immediately saw the movement and with a giant leap disappeared into the brush.

# Hagenbeck's Lynx

I stood there, numb. But then, just to the right, something reddish. The gun came up, aiming for a small opening ahead. A brief glimpse of the target and the gun roared. Then silence, only ravens calling.

Could I hope that such a quickly thrown shot had hit its mark? The hounds stormed out of the brush, overshooting where the lynx had appeared; a quick retrace, then back on the trail to again disappear. I raced after them. They hunted on for another thirty metres or so, then silence. They came towards me. 'Where is he?' I urged them to follow and ran another ten steps or so and stopped. In front of me was the lynx, its tongue bitten through. The hounds dropped beside it without touching it.

I was just about to blow the signal 'all dead' when the Karelian appeared. He began to examine the lynx and rolled it over. 'Ah, a mature female. Look here, she's had young – probably still with her.'

'All the better!' I said. 'We can continue with the hunt tomorrow.'

'That's what you think! Now we know where they are we can come back in two months on skis and catch them alive.'

I could see this might turn into an argument and so suggested we skin the lynx and get something to eat. Without answering, he pulled out his knife, cut off a long slender birch branch and, putting a foot on one end, proceeded to twist it into a 'rope' to hang the animal up with. And all of this with one hand.

'Would you like some help with the skinning?' I asked. He didn't respond, irritated I'm sure by the clash of opinions. 'All right, I'll start supper and coffee then.'

'Six of those little birds for me,' he mumbled, turning his back to me. 'But that'll be the last of them for me on this silly trip. Tomorrow I'm going to shoot a capercaillie, a proper bird with some meat on it. I've had enough of nibbling away like an insect.'

With his desire for something more substantial, I suggested we try a joint from the lynx, something I'd once seen on the menu of a fine restaurant in Helsinki.

'You might like cat meat, but not me! I'm not that hard up yet, despite your efforts to get me there.'

Later that evening having eaten our 'little birds', we sat around the campfire when he began, 'I suppose you believe the earth spins around the sun, and not the other way around.' He may not have belonged to the 'flat earth society' but he wasn't far off. He steadfastly refused to discuss anything to do with Copernicus, though I don't believe he'd ever heard of him or his teachings.

'But surely you don't believe the dead can cross water?' The belief was that the dead could not cross water and so were best buried on islands; indeed, the district we were hunting had such an island cemetery. It was called the Island of the Dead and sat in the middle of a lake. Small log houses covered the graves, their shingled roofs – those that hadn't collapsed – thickly coated with moss. These huts provided shelter for the souls of the dead. Small bowls with various spices, herbs and tobacco were placed in them and when mice and birds had emptied them it was thought the dead had celebrated.

It was this island my friend was referring to as he continued, 'Well, with the cemetery on the island full, they've now built one on the mainland. What's even worse is that along with this nonsense has come the habit of not putting shelters over the graves. My mother was a mourner at the funeral of Ontrei's wife, who was buried in the new cemetery. After the funeral the dead lady visited my mother's house every night until she nearly went out of her mind.'

'Did anyone see the dead woman?' I was getting tired.

'Yes, but mainly it was her smell. Every morning the house smelt as if you had skinned a dozen weasels in it. I'm telling you: the dead have to be buried on islands. That's the way it has always been.' And with that we both turned in.

Next morning I unleashed the hounds while having my coffee and wandered a little way into the forest with them. With little arousing their interest I left them loose and returned to the fire and breakfast. The Karelian and I had barely started our meal when the bitch hound gave out a great howl – the hunt was on!

I grabbed my gun, but my friend halted me. 'Nobody should go to work on an empty stomach.'

'Hunting isn't exactly work to me,' and I grabbed a cold grouse and was off.

The hunt was playing out within hearing distance. I was sure it involved a hare and took a position close to where the lynx had been shot. The hunt came close but the hare remained in thick cover, not showing itself once. I changed position and held my new post for a while, but the hunt had moved further to the east, still following a typical hare-style pattern.

I moved again, finding a good hare run on the edge of a birch-covered hillock. At one point the hunt passed me within a hundred metres, but with the pursuit following a gully thickly covered on both sides by small firs, I saw nothing. I went to the gully and stayed put.

The hunt now came right at me, drawing closer and closer. Then total astonishment: the tones coming through the forest signalled that the hounds had forced their quarry to take refuge in a tree – which of course made nonsense of my hare theory.

I ran for all I was worth, homing in on the dog hound; from the bitch there wasn't a sound. There's nothing more exciting than knowing your hounds have treed game, especially when that game might be a lynx. But was he in a tree or had he decided to stand his ground on a stump or boulder? No, he had to be in a tree or the hound would have sounded far more excited.

Finally I was on the scene. The dog hound was sitting under a thick pine, while the bitch hurried back and forth, whining and repeatedly casting glances at the tree. And there was the lynx, right above them and seemingly unperturbed by it all. As it saw me, it climbed higher, going almost to the top where it sat tight against the trunk. I leashed both hounds so they wouldn't run in on the lynx when I shot it: often such an animal has enough life left in it to cause a great deal of damage.

In the low light of autumn, the lynx made a wonderful sight, its gleaming coat competing fiercely with the amber-red cones of the pine. I raised my gun but was abruptly stopped by the Karelian who had come up unnoticed.

'A rabid fox must have bitten you; there won't be any shooting here. At least not at the lynx! I'll bring this prize down alive.'

'And just how are you going to do that with your stump?' I

inquired, a bit amused by the thought.

'Never you mind. I'm taking him alive. Release the hounds again.'

With that, he produced two leather straps, each having a snare at one end. He threw down his jacket, took one of the straps in his mouth and began to climb. As he neared the lynx it climbed higher, but running out of tree it soon had to stop. I don't know how he managed it, but somehow the Karelian held himself in the tree with his stump arm and slowly put the snare around the lynx's back leg and pulled it tight. The lynx erupted, made a massive leap wrenching my companion from the tree, and the two of them came crashing down through the thick branches. As they landed – the Karelian falling on top of the lynx – there was a tearing, ripping commotion and within seconds the lynx was racing through the timber, the hounds in pursuit.

My companion rose quickly. He was in good spirit but a sorry state! His chest was severely scratched and cut about and his clothes were in tatters. He removed his shirt, which was hanging loose like some old rag, turned it around and pulled it back on, the back now facing front, and knotted the rest of his clothing together as best he could, all the time screaming frightful obscenities but grinning happily!

He'd hardly finished when the hounds broke into a song that told me the lynx was once again in a tree. We rushed in their direction.

We arrived to an almost comical spectacle. The lynx had climbed a small thin birch that had bent right over under its weight, leaving the poor cat barely four metres above the ground and hanging upside down. The strap, still attached to its back leg, was easily within reach. 'Now we've got him,' said my companion, and tore off his jacket. 'I'll pull the tree down a bit more, then you secure the strap, throw my jacket over his head and get hold of his front feet. I'll do the rest.'

The plan didn't appeal to me at all but as soon as the lynx was low enough I put the coat over his head. He hung on for a second or so then leapt from the tree. Both of us were quickly on top of him, the Karelian moving swiftly to bind his legs. As he worked, the furious lynx attempted to bite me through the coat. 'Don't let go!' roared my companion, emptying his rucksack. 'Just hold him down and I'll stuff the pack over his head.'

As he tried to do this one of the animal's front feet came free. He grabbed this but in the process received a bad bite in his arm. It was all a bit chaotic but somehow we managed to get the cat's legs properly tied and the animal itself in the rucksack – where it sat, just its head protruding, observing us with its incredibly beautiful eyes. 'There,' the Karelian said happily, shaking the blood from his arm and hand. 'Now we've got him.' Yes we had, but we'd been very lucky. Our lynx was a young animal. Had we been dealing with an adult, things might have had a less happy outcome.

After we'd eaten – and my companion had once again tied his rags together – we stowed all our gear in the free rucksack, hung the lynx-pack on a pole between us, and set off for the nearest village in triumph. We spent the darkest hours sitting by a campfire, but as soon as the moon came up we continued and by dawn came to a house. The lynx was put into a quickly made crate and by evening was dining on a capercaillie we'd shot.

A week later found us heading for home aboard a two-wheeled cart. My friend was in excellent humour, largely due to the fact that we had sold the lynx to the Hagenbeck's agent for two hundred and fifty marks. He'd treated himself to a bottle of something lethal and had nearly finished it. 'I think I'll have myself buried on the mainland,' he slurred. 'Then I can wander into town now and again to get a drop of this wonderful stuff.' And with that he slowly slid onto the floor of the cart and fell fast asleep.

# 5
# Forester Backman and the Lynx Runners

My father died in June 1906. He was barely forty-seven years old. The mine had been sold to the Putislov Works a little earlier – my father having stayed on as manager – and so, with little to keep us in the district, we moved to Helsinki where the family owned a big apartment building in Kronohagen, the most exclusive part of town.

I had graduated from high school and wanted to go into forestry. With the state owning vast tracts of forest, it was a common profession, if perhaps more out of need than real desire, the pay being very poor. For me the appeal was its link to the wilderness: I'd suffer the low wages for the chance to live alongside nature.

To acquaint myself with my new profession I was to spend a winter with Nils Backman, an old friend of my fathers who ran a forestry operation at Uomala, some one hundred and fifty kilometres north-east of Lake Ladoga.*

*This appears to be the same forester Remmler mentions in his cockerel story (chapter three).

So, one late-autumn evening I took the train from Helsinki to Sortavala, travelling on by horse next morning to the village of Kitelä where I stayed overnight in a guesthouse. The horse cart to take me to Uomala had been reserved in advance and I was to continue early next morning. In the Finnish provinces (and in the provinces of Sweden, Norway and Russia) travel always involved guesthouse horses. There was a standard charge for the horses plus a fee for every kilometre travelled. Your driver was required to do about ten kilometres per hour: more couldn't be expected. In the more populated areas, a guesthouse could be relied upon every twenty kilometres. However, in more remote districts this distance could be double or more and under these conditions the traveller was better off buying a horse and selling it at his destination.

I arrived in Uomala to find that the good forester Backman had taken God's advice to Adam and Eve – 'Go forth and multiply' – literally. A mouse wouldn't have found a bed. He apologised for not being able to put me up. But there was truly nothing he could do, especially as another child was due any day! I felt almost obliged to tell him that God had not intended that he alone should see to all the multiplying, but kept quiet. It was a desire to please the Lord that had obviously been inherited. His father had left fifteen children behind at his death. Apparently, when asked how many children he had he used to say, 'I'm not sure, but I know them all when I see them.'

With no space at the forester's, I took a room at the widow Oanan's house some three kilometres away and skied to work each day.

My initial post at Backman's was office work. I hated it. The drudgery of filling in forms and charts was unbearable but it was something my terrible handwriting soon saved me from. My employer was most particular about presentation and the sight of my hideous scribble against his beautifully neat hand had me outdoors posthaste. Here I was occupied with 'stamping'. Every tree to be felled required two stamps, one close to the ground, which remained on the stump, and another, about two metres higher, that would go with the felled log. Twelve of us would ski out each day and use our axes to put the royal crown on every tree intended for the pulp industry. My role was to help the forester seek out trees to be saved for seeding, which of course wouldn't be stamped.

Amongst the forest workers was a woman who used a hand-pulled sledge to drag timber out of the forest to where the horses could take over. She was heavily pregnant and one day didn't show up for work. The next morning a young lad arrived telling us that the woman was near death. Within minutes I had been elected to fetch the doctor – no easy mission as he lived a good fifty kilometres away and the roads were heavily snowed in. Somehow I made it, left my own exhausted horse there, and headed back with the doctor, using a fresh animal from his stable. We were at the woman's little hut by dawn.

After a quick examination the doctor decided he would have to use forceps to bring the baby into the world and demanded boiling water to sterilise the instruments. It turned out there was only one pot in the whole house and it was full to the brim with rye-meal porridge. The doctor, who was no stranger to wilderness deliveries, lost nether patience or humour.

'Good,' he said, 'we'll have some porridge first!' And at that, all of us – the doctor, myself and five children – gathered around the pot with wooden spoons and ate away until the bottom began to show.

After the instruments had been sterilised the doctor decided he needed an assistant and promptly showed me how to hold the woman's legs so that she wouldn't fall off the table when he pulled. Her children stood round dumbfounded: anyone later attempting to tell them the story of the stork was going to find himself faced with a very sceptical audience!

The doctor may not have been well versed in the higher areas of surgery but in no time at all he had the baby's head in the forceps and delivered it as neatly as pulling a beet out of the ground.

I now had hold of the baby, which made not a sound and appeared dead. 'Quick, stick its arse in the snow!' the doctor instructed. My second's hesitation had one of the older children grab the baby and rush outside, and soon the newborn was howling away. We'd done it!

I hadn't been in my new job long when a group of us – my

employer included – found ourselves working away from home. A paper mill had purchased a large amount of pulpwood on the stump and been given permission to do its own cutting as long as this was done under the watchful eyes of state forestry employees.

The weather had turned exceptionally cold – so cold in fact that forester Backman had deemed it too cold to work. Well, too cold for work it might have been but not too cold for me to go hunting. So after breakfast I grabbed my skis and set out to see if I could shoot a ptarmigan or two. I'd always been a keen ptarmigan hunter and had spent much time learning their ways. In winter they were usually found at the edge of the forest or along brooks where birch and willow bushes grew. They fed on the buds from these bushes and leapt high into the air to get them. Hunters saw this behaviour as a weathervane; the higher the ptarmigan leapt, the poorer the weather was going to be.

Half an hour later I was deep in the forest. It was deadly quiet as is so often the case in winter when very cold. I was gliding down a slope when the snow left and right of me suddenly exploded. It was like landmines going off as about thirty black grouse were on the wing and

away. By the time I'd got my gun from over my back, they were long out of range. I was startled by the eruption but had experienced similar encounters many times before. Forest grouse, especially black grouse and ptarmigan, often seek protection from the cold by burrowing into snow – sometimes for many metres. If surprised they burst out going straight up through the snow rather than exit via the burrow.

The grouse gone, I now began to search for ptarmigan. Having hunted them since childhood, I was quite skilled at spotting them. Against a backdrop of snow their white plumage granted them wonderful camouflage but their little black eyes gave the game away. Near a feeding spot I found eight sets of tracks heading towards an area of open moor. Going with the gradient I slid slowly on, ski sticks tucked under my belt and gun at the ready, all the while scanning the snow for those black eyes.

Twenty steps ahead, a ptarmigan suddenly grew out of the snow, tipped his tail and ran. Before I'd got my gun up, it had been joined by seven more – all now on the wing. I brought two down with the first shot; whether the second barrel had hit anything I couldn't tell.

I quickly picked up the downed birds and followed. I'd just spied a head sticking up out of the snow when the covey flushed again, out of range. Chasing after them as quickly as was possible without ski sticks, I noticed that one had obviously been hit. It circled and fell. By the time I got to it, death was seconds away.

On the way home I shot a hare. Our landlady – we were staying at a farm – took the three ptarmigan but wanted nothing to do with the hare – which didn't surprise me. Farmers and other land workers in northern and eastern parts of Finland would never eat hare. In fact, at the large fur auctions a white hare pelt would bring ten marks, but an entire animal would only fetch nine. One mark was deducted for the need to skin it!

That afternoon we sat in the main room of the farmhouse. It was the room in which everything was done, cooking, eating, sewing – even carpentry. This was quite normal in the more remote areas. The maids and hired hands slept in this room, and even the older children. Sometimes even a horse would be allowed in if the weather turned severe enough and there was no room in the stable; even hens, calves and piglets might be accommodated. Thus you might find yourself answering the call of nature in the night to stumble over a piglet or find a hen flutter up onto your head!

'There they are,' said the little blonde girl sitting at the window combing her hair with a small, tight-toothed 'louse-rake'.

I looked out and saw two men getting out of a sleigh. The horse that pulled it was astonishing. It was covered with hair more resembling that of a Tibetan yak than a horse. It was so long it hung down to almost touch the ground.

Our landlady's husband went out to help unharness the 'yak' and stable it. This done, the men began to rummage about in the sleigh, bringing out a bundle of boards. 'Who are they?' I asked our landlady.

'Who are they?' She looked at me as if I'd gone mad. 'That's Pekka Ikonen with his new partner, Koponen.'

Now I understood the reverence in her voice: Pekka Ikonen was one of the most famous lynx runners in all Karelia. Backman glanced at me over the top of his book: serious company indeed!

The men entered the room, offered a short greeting and dropped their boards on the floor. I went outside to take a look at their skis. Not only were they incredibly beautiful, they were perfect for running in deep powdered snow. They were fairly short, conspicuously broad and had a wide groove in the middle. They were also whisper thin and so flexible it was almost beyond belief.

I came back in to find our guests enjoying a meal. Using their hunting knives, they were slicing great slabs off a dark rye loaf, covering them with butter and adding a thick slice of salted raw salmon. It was simple fare but went down with clear enjoyment.

After eating they began to hammer a crate together. It was obviously for a lynx and one of my co-workers couldn't resist commenting, 'Wouldn't it be better to first catch the lynx then make the crate?'

Without looking up, Ikonen replied, 'You may be the type who buys a horse then builds a stable, we do things the other way around.'

The next day we left the lynx hunters preparing their gear and set off for work. It was an uneventful day except for an incident on our return journey.

We'd come to a huge moor at least four or five kilometres across. About five hundred metres out was a group of small pines and in them I spied perhaps thirty roosting capercaillie, who always preferred the yellowish needles of small moor-growing pines to the darker needles of those growing on better soil. I had my Sports Mauser with me, and the forester, halting us, suggested I try my luck. It was a proposal delivered with a grin to the other men and I knew he thought I was about to make a complete fool of myself.

Keeping well hidden, I followed the edge of the moor trying to get as close as possible to my quarry. I was lucky and got to a good spot without disturbing anything to give the game away. I lay down and supported the rifle on a log. My ammunition was perfect. Over the years I'd learned to reverse the bullets in their casings so that the pointed tip faced backwards. Many a time I'd shot straight through a capercaillie without inflicting any damage. A reversed bullet brought them down every time.

In one of the larger pines were eight birds with their heads pulled in tight. They felt safe; I didn't have to hurry. As soon as I had assured myself that the bird I was aiming at was the lowest one in the tree, I fired. As my reversed bullet went home it looked as if the bird had simply jumped off the branch into the snow. The others didn't move, the crack of the rifle not bothering them at all: on a cold day the forest is full of such sounds, the crack of ice on a lake or frost in the trees. The important thing is to always shoot the lowest bird. Beginners often pick the most prominent bird – the one sitting at the top of the tree – but when it falls, possibly hitting one of its companions on the way down, the rest take flight.

I shot again, this time aiming at the next bird up, and brought it down too. Then two more. By which time I was pretty sure I'd proved my point: a blundering novice I wasn't. And anyway, a fully-grown capercaillie weighs as much as four kilos, some birds making as much as six. With the prospect of carrying them home by myself, four was enough.

After binding the birds together in pairs, I made my way back to the

others.

'I see those weren't your first huurumetsos,' the forester said with a laugh. He then generously took two of the birds from me and we headed for home.

Huurumetso (hoarfrost capercaillie) is just one of the names the capercaillie has, its title altering with the time of year and whether it is male or female. The wealth of descriptive words the wilderness people of the north have is truly amazing. The Lapps for instance have no actual word for slope – but they have eleven different words to describe it: steep, shallow, covered in birch, moss, or even if it is facing north or south. One word will tell you all you needed to know.

We arrived home to find the crate empty and the lynx hunters sprawled out on the floor. To question them would have been totally inappropriate – and unnecessary. Anyone with eyes and ears could see how things stood.

In addition to the lynx hunters, two new guests had arrived. They were foresters who had been sent by head office to relieve Backman so he could attend the funeral of some relative. It was a journey of three hundred kilometres and he was due to leave within the hour. This now forced my hand. On seeing the empty crate, I'd planned to wait for the right moment and ask permission to join the lynx hunters. Now I had to act immediately and just came out with it. His response caught me off guard.

'And if I say no, what then!' But his face broke into a smile. 'I was wondering how long it was going to take for you to ask!'

I'd won the first battle but how was I going to handle the lynx hunters? How to convince them I would be an asset? Maybe I'd have to be a little sly.

Later that evening I sat down with the new foresters and deliberately steered the conversation so that I could mention knowing the general district due to a lynx hunt I'd been on. They were intrigued and I was ready to elaborate, laying out the whole tale, my disabled companion, the treed cat – and our success. That was all it took. The two trappers came over.

'So all that stuff one-handed Jashka has been bragging about is true,' said Ikonen. 'He did take the lynx out of the tree. Nobody wanted to believe the old windbag.'

'Why do you call him a windbag?' I asked.

'Well look what a laughing stock he made of himself with that bear. Too bad young Vornanen has become involved with him. The Vornanens are some of the most respected hunters in all Karelia – and Finland.' (Even though Karelia was part of Finland, border inhabitants saw it as a foreign country. It came from the fact that all through the Swedish times Karelia had belonged to Russia and was only joined to the Motherland after the lost war of 1809.)

'Well, that's as maybe but he certainly has guts. As far as I know only Auvonen has ever managed to take a lynx out of a tree.'

'You are wrong there, Ryökäs has done it as well.'

'Could be,' I said, 'but I still consider Jashka an excellent hunting companion, even if he does drink more than he should. It's not often I've shared a campfire with more entertaining company.'

'You're right there,' laughed Ikonen. 'He's a good man, as long as you don't take him too seriously!'

At this point I considered asking to join them on their lynx hunt, but decided not to. I was worried they might think they were doing me some great favour, and that I didn't want. It would be much better to have things the other way around. So I resumed my conversation steering, finally ending up at wolf hunting where I could casually tell them all about my experiences with the Kazakhs.

'You have an eagle like that!' exclaimed Ikonen.

'Yes, he's in Uomais, at the forester's place. His children are catching hares for him while I'm away.'

'Well I'll be damned. Say, how would you like to join us on our hunt?'

I'd got my invitation!

Following a rather meagre breakfast, next morning we were on our way, Koponen leading, then Ikonen, with me trailing slightly. The pace was fairly easy, the kind of tempo you'd expect from a man geared to do at least forty kilometres a day. We were following the lynx trail they'd been on the day before: they'd chased the lynx for about twenty

minutes and then given up because they hadn't been able to gain on it. In about an hour we arrived at where they'd quit and now followed the trail at a leisurely pace. Looking at the previous day's tracks you could clearly see that the lynx had immediately registered it was no longer being chased and slowed down. A little later we even found a spot where it had settled down to rest, the tracks then continuing at a walk.

Shortly afterwards we came to a small valley that ran down to a stream. The lynx had crouched on the slope then made several huge leaps – each covering nearly ten metres. He'd been hunting a hare, which he'd caught and eaten it on the spot. It was now clear that the chase would soon be on: our lynx wouldn't be going far on a full stomach. Ikonen now took the lead.

The tension grew with every metre, nerves and excitement causing my palms to sweat. What seemed like an age passed when suddenly the snow in front exploded and something yellowish disappeared into the trees.

Ikonen's coat flew past my head, then his cap. Koponen wasn't quite as fast, but he too was soon without coat and hat and roaring after Ikonen. In the trail they left behind, the skiing was easier for me but I still had to give my all to keep up.

The men were yelling as loudly as possible to keep the lynx running. Branches hit my face, snow went down my neck and my cap was left somewhere in the forest but I registered none of it as we raced hell for leather down a steep slope.

'We've got him!' yelled Ikonen. 'See to it he doesn't swing left or right.'

Koponen broke one way, I the other. But within moments Ikonen had caught up with the lynx, got his ski sticks in a cross over it and was pressing it into the snow so deeply it was almost buried. Koponen offered the snarling animal the standard ski stick and glove and took some leather snares out of his pocket. The binding of the animal was conducted so deftly I was astonished.

The men now hurried; it was bitterly cold and they'd discarded all but their shirts during the chase. The lynx was loaded into a bag Koponen produced from under his belt, leaving only its head sticking out. The bundle was then tied to a pole and we set off heading back in our own tracks.

Having found their clothes we stopped for a rest. I'd found my own cap too and put it on. It was like a chunk of ice. Their clothes must have been the same but they didn't seem to register it and no one suggested lighting a fire.

On the way home we were accompanied by several 'bad luck birds', whose calls, as their name suggests, were thought to bring bad luck. We also passed a little pygmy owl peacefully eating a small bird. It was so close I could have touched it.

Back at the farmhouse the lynx was put in the crate and offered a hare, which it refused. The following morning Koponen and Ikonen left with their prize; it was unlikely they would return that winter.

# 6
# The Maisula Wolf

A month after the lynx hunt we moved back to Uomais where I continued to board with the widow Oanan. One evening I returned home to find she had another lodger, a young man equipped with a cheap single-shot shotgun and a black and white spitz. He was on his way to Maisula where there had been several sightings of a wolf. He had ski-chased wolves before in this general area but they'd always escaped across the border. Maisula's location however gave him hope of being more successful.

I knew Maisula, or more accurately its filthy and dilapidated guest-house. During a hunt I'd once ended up there with my brother. We were starving but still thought long and hard about what might be safe to order. We eventually decided on eggs. Which was a pity because the landlady only had bread, salted fish and buttermilk. Okay, bread and fish it would be. This duly arrived but without cutlery. We had our hunting knives but tried to explain that we'd like forks for the fish. For some reason she couldn't understand what I meant. So I tried to demonstrate with spread fingers.

'Ah, vilka, vilka!' she exclaimed, using the Russian for fork, and rushed off to fetch something that at one time might have indeed been a fork. It had no handle, one of its three prongs was missing and it was filthy! I pointed out how dirty it was, at which she spat on it and wiped it with the hem of her dress. Before I could save them, our cups suf-

fered the same fate!

That was the guesthouse in Maisula.

While we'd been talking I'd been eying up the stranger's dog. I'd long wanted one of these Karelian bear dogs and pondered how I might acquire it. To simply offer cash would have been totally unacceptable; things just weren't done that way out here. Some kind of swap would be much more likely to succeed, and looking at his cheap gun I had the perfect item.

'Do you need the dog for your wolf hunt?' I asked; he was now by the fire tarring his skis.

'No,' he said and I grabbed my hammered double barrel and handed it to him.

'Here, take this, and the dog's mine.' His eyes wandered from gun to dog – and back again.

'A good trade,' he said. 'Shake!'

'So, what's your name?' I inquired.

'Korhonen,' he replied.

'Not THE Korhonen! Korhonen, the famous hunter?' I'd pictured him much older. But it was him and, still tarring his skis, he began to tell of hunts that held me spellbound. As his wolves, campfires and chases through the pines took us into the early hours, I was determined to join him on his mission to Maisula.

Next morning I skied over to the forester's place and asked if I could be spared. He had no objections and so I rushed back to make preparations for the long hunt: Odin would be provided for as before and the widow promised to look after my newly acquired dog.

Remembering the Maisula guesthouse I packed butter, ham and cheese. Korhonen supplied a cooking pot, axe and the vital matches. The latter were in a holder made from a ram's scrotum. He insisted this was waterproof – and I hoped he was right. On this kind of winter hunt it was quite possible to fall through ice and become totally saturated. If this happened, the precious matches and the fire they could provide were the only thing between you and freezing to death. I always tended to keep a well-sealed rubber bag in the bottom of my rucksack, which held not only matches but spare trousers and a shirt. I looked at his match pouch again and packed my own.

Unlike lynx hunting, speed skiing is not the way to run down a wolf. Only perseverance and toughness bring results. The hunter must be able to spend nights out and be able to get some proper rest rather than just shiver through the night. It's a highly demanding type of hunt and few can cope with the hardship it brings; for those more accustomed to living within four walls, it's an impossible challenge. I was fully aware of this, but undaunted: I was young and fit and had skied from a very early age. I would see it through no matter what lay ahead.

It was shockingly cold when we departed – minus 32°C. The widow tried desperately to dissuade me, and my boss had sent word that I should under no circumstances go. It was a message that came too late and with me fired up and prepared, probably wouldn't have stopped me anyway.

I was kitted out in full Lapp or Sami dress made almost entirely from reindeer hide. The main body of the outfit was a long thick pullover top called a peski, which took no less than six hides to make. A colourful band was tied around the waist and then the coat was pulled up so that it ballooned into a wide blouse around the upper body. It was an ingenious invention, the air pocket giving far better insulation than any sweater or other woollen item. On my feet I wore boots – more socks really – made of shorthaired hide. These were accompanied by gaiters fashioned from leg hide and where gaiter met boot, a red woollen band called the paulanauha was tied. My headgear was the traditional 'four winds' cap, a down-filled hat of reindeer skin with a four-pointed top. Decorated with colourful bands, such an outfit might seem too bright for the wilderness, but in fact it blends perfectly and is the ideal hunting attire. A Laplander dressed this way is at one with nature, like a fox or a wolf. A man in a grey coat will simply be a man in a grey coat and never blend into the surroundings.

We stayed on the great Uukus River, which flows past Maisula and Uomais to Lake Ladoga. Skiing was far easier on the snow-covered ice than in the bush.

A winter's day in the north is short, and it wasn't long before we had to prepare for the night. We sought out a large Kelohonka, an ancient pine that had fallen many years after its death. Such a tree has a trunk so saturated with pitch that the wood will burn almost as if it had been soaked in oil. Our Kelohonka found, we set about preparing a fire, splitting a three-metre-long section to construct something that would burn all night without being touched. A bed of spruce branches each side of the fire and our 'room' was ready.

Above us the trails of falling stars came and disappeared, the fire spat and sparkled sending up tiny sparks quickly doused by the snow, the moon, the colour of a marten's throat patch, stood high above, and in the distance the ghostly veils of the northern lights rushed across the sky. I pulled my blanket around me and dozed off.

When I awoke next morning, Korhonen already had the tea on the go and we settled down to a good breakfast. The conversation leant very much towards the commercial value of our mission. Korhonen was a dedicated hunter, but he wasn't in it for pleasure. For him it was all business and before he undertook any hunting excursion he calculated exactly whether it was worth the trouble and what the profit would be. I'd realised this back in Uomais and used it as a way of get-

ting him to invite me. Rather than demanding a fifty-fifty share, I assured him that anything we bagged would be his alone. Without this guarantee I'd have had no chance of joining him.

We broke camp and set out. To share the burden of skiing through unbroken snow, each took a turn leading. In the afternoon I was leading when we crossed a trail. One glance was enough: a wolf.

'I imagine this is the Maisula wolf,' I said to Korhonen who had stopped behind me.

'Looks like it. Let's hope he's not heading east for the border.'

We followed the trail slowly; we had no intention of starting the pursuit today, we just wanted to find out what the wolf's plans were.

We came to a spot where he'd stumbled into a black grouse. He'd eaten it immediately and then headed northwest. We were in luck. We followed the trail for another couple of kilometres then stopped at a small lake where we decided to camp. We made tea, had some food and began to prepare for the night, this time building two fires and putting our bedding between them. This way we weren't freezing on one side while roasting on the other.

Long before daybreak we began to get ready for the chase ahead. We had a hearty breakfast and drank lots of tea, discovering in the process that our supplies were low and we would need to secure something to eat before evening, which was far from ideal.

Backpacks were arranged so that nothing would rattle while we were chasing and gun slings were rearranged so that our weapons could be carried with their barrels pointing down; the trees were so heavily laden with snow that the barrels would have been full of snow in no time had we left them in the usual position.

It was hard to tell how old the trail was but we believed it might take most of the day to catch our wolf up. We were right: the trail remained cold all day. We found a place where he had been mousing, and also where he'd dug out a couple of weasels. Then we came to the scene of a more substantial kill – he'd chased down a fox and consumed everything bar a few bits of pelt. With his belly full, he would probably be sleeping not too far away. But evening was already with us and so we made camp and shared a black grouse Korhonen had shot earlier. It wasn't much for two hungry men but it would have to do.

Next morning the weather had changed. It had turned much warmer and the sky was promising snow. That's all we needed, fresh snow to wipe out the tracks!

With lots of tea doing a poor job of fending off hunger, we were soon on the trail and about two kilometres later found where the wolf had spent the night. He'd left long ago. On we went.

Despite having consumed a whole fox, our wolf was once again hunting: in a clearing he'd been mousing again and on a snow bank he'd surprised a grouse. After the grouse he'd turned west and arrived at a small lake, which he'd crossed. We followed, but on the opposite shore his tracks altered: he'd moved into a run. He'd noticed he was being followed.

'We can't continue like this,' I said. 'We'll have to get something to eat. You follow the trail and I'll stay behind and try for a few ptarmigan along the shoreline.' A glance, and my companion was gone.

To the north, the sky looked ominous: yes, snow was definitely on the way and promising to come as a storm. I should have asked Korhonen for the axe, but it was too late now. I loaded my gun with smaller shot and began the search along the shore. I hoped the coming weather would help me: when a storm is imminent, ptarmigan are generally so intent on feeding they are more approachable. However, as is so often the case, the more urgent the mission, the slower things seem to move.

Finally I spotted about fifteen birds jumping busily after buds. I raised the gun, waited until I had as many as possible lined up, then fired, immediately following up on two other birds with the second barrel. I reloaded and hurried to the spot. I'd hit four of them.

I picked up the ptarmigan and went looking for the wolf tracks, and of course Korhonen's. My little hunt had taken nearly two hours and now dark clouds covered half the sky. It was going to snow any minute. I skied as fast as I could, but already the first few flakes were falling and the wind was picking up.

I pushed on. Amongst the trees the trail was still quite easy to follow, but I knew that out on the moors and lakes it would be impossible; indeed the way the storm was looking, I wouldn't be able to see anything at all. After two hours of running I gave up. There was no sense in killing myself. I had matches, a compass and my large Lapp knife. Without the axe I wouldn't be able to build a proper fire but I'd be able to get something going.

Not far away I found a big dead pine. The way it was lying offered me pretty good protection for the night and would also shelter my fire. I started breaking off branches, which proved tough work due to their thickness. However, I eventually had a good supply and with slivers cut from these and the whole thing piled against the main log, all I had to do now was try and get a flame started. If I couldn't achieve this I was going to be in serious trouble. I have to confess, I was worried.

Suddenly I spied a dark shape moving swiftly through the trees. I yelled as loud as I could but the storm carried my voice away. I frantically grabbed my gun and let off both barrels. Nothing. I went for my skis: the dark shape I'd seen had to be Korhonen; maybe I could find him. It was either that or spend the night here alone. And at that exact moment, he appeared.

'That was a close call,' he said. 'I heard the shots.' He'd turned back as soon as the storm began.

When he spotted the ptarmigan his eyes widened and he immediately began skinning them; plucking was something we didn't have time for. I grabbed the axe and got busy building a proper fire.

Next morning the sky was clear and the wind had dropped somewhat. However, we gazed out over twenty centimetres of fresh track-burying snow. I could see Korhonen wasn't happy.

'Now what?' he said, without getting up.

'We'll finish what we started, that's what. Or have you had enough already? We'll head straight west until we either pick up the trail or hit the road to Suojarvi. In the latter case we'll stay in Maisula, get some supplies, and then look around until we find the trail again.' I knew my tone was overstepping the mark a bit but I felt sure that without my clear enthusiasm the hunt might be over.

'Okay,' he said, but the reluctance in his voice was obvious.

We skied west all day not seeing so much as a hare track. Not a paw had broken the new blanket of snow and it seemed every scrap of life had gone into hiding – except for the chirpy forest tits who were as busy as ever. They couldn't survive a day without food.

At dusk we reached the road to Suojarvi and an hour later we were taking our skis off at the Maisula guesthouse.

The place had improved a great deal. The previous owner had been resting in the cemetery for a year and her daughter-in-law had taken over the business. Not only did the place now boast proper cutlery, it even supplied clean guest towels. The mattresses were still filled with nothing but straw and lay flat on the bare floor, but the new owner promised there would be no lice in them – only bed bugs and fleas! Well what did we expect, the St. Petersburg Winter Palace?

After eating we settled down to keep the bed bugs company and slept well into the following morning. At breakfast the man of the house came in: he'd seen wolf tracks crossing the road less than three kilometres to the south. We were on our skis and away.

'That's our wolf,' I announced as we came to the tracks.

'I hope so,' Korhonen said and he began to follow the trail across an open moor. The tracks were fresh and within an hour the wolf was running ahead of us. By evening we were near the village of Teronvaara; it lay some twenty-five kilometres northwest of Maisula but we had skied probably twice that distance. We broke off the hunt and set course for the house of a man Korhonen knew. We were there in half an hour. After food and plenty of tea we retired for the night – our first proper beds since starting out.

At first light we were on the wolf's trail again. He had gone in a southwesterly direction and caught and eaten a dog on the outskirts of a village. With this kill having been the night before, he was now not only well fed but well rested – not the best news for us.

We stayed on his trail all day – only halting when it became too dark to see it – and before dawn we were after him again. This we kept up for three days. On the fourth day we saw him for the first time; he was running across a lake about a kilometre away. This gave us a burst of enthusiasm and we sped up; but there was no chance of catching him and soon he was out of sight on the far shore.

Suddenly Korhonen yelled, 'Stop!' There was water on top of the ice along the shoreline – something he'd failed to notice due to our haste. I was some way back and managed to halt in time but for Korhonen it was too late, his skis were iced up. He came paddling towards me swearing and cursing. We both knew this was going to cost time because while it would be possible to scrape the ice off, to dry his skis and get them fully functional would require a fire.

'I'll stay on the trail and you catch up as soon as you can,' I said.

He nodded, and I was off. My aim was to catch up with the wolf myself – and I gave the pursuit my all. But it was useless: all day at the task and I couldn't bring him to a run. I halted and made camp long before the stars were out so as not to load Korhonen with more trouble than he already had.

I waited huddled by the fire, but darkness eventually fell with still no sign of him. Tired, I lay down and fell asleep. The fire was nearly out when he awakened me. I glanced at my watch. It was two o'clock. He was in a frightful mood. Having sorted his skis out, he'd gone no more than a hundred metres when he broke the tip off one of them! He'd then returned to the fire and tried to form a new bend in the broken tip, but while achieving something better than he had, the ski was useless for chasing wolves.

Next morning we set course for Maisula, heading east in the direction of Suojarvi to find the Uukus River. We followed this to Lake Salmi, eventually hitting the road about three kilometres north of our goal. It was midnight by the time we arrived and, bathed in moonlight, the guesthouse was a welcome if slightly eerie sight. We slept like the dead.

In the morning Korhonen declared he'd had enough. He was going grouse hunting instead. A bit of bargaining with the landlady got him a pair of skis and he was soon on his way.

So now I was on my own. To go after the wolf single-handed would have been difficult as well as risky: an accident and I'd have been in serious trouble. There was nothing for it but to return to Uomais.

More than a little fed up, I sat staring into the fire. I heard the door open but thinking it must be the landlady, didn't look up until I heard a

deep male voice. 'Greetings young man.' I looked up and met the smiling eyes of a man in his mid-thirties. Without any invitation he pulled up a chair and began to chat in an oddly free manner. It soon became clear he knew a lot more about me than I did of him.

'So you're the fellow with the eagle, the one who took the lynx with Jashka.' He must have talked with Ikonen and Koponen. 'And now you are here to try your luck running down a wolf.' I was on the verge of becoming a little irritated at his nosiness when he finally introduced himself – he was the great lynx hunter Heikki Auvonen! I seemed destined to meet every famous hunter in Finland!

Auvonen had heard about our failed hunt and decided to see if I wanted some help. I was, to use his words, 'clearly more than your average brat.' I of course welcomed his involvement with open arms and we immediately struck a deal: I would get the pelt; he would claim the bounty.

In the afternoon it clouded over and began to snow, and continued to do so for two days without pause. We slept, ate and sat by the fire, where the landlady's husband amused us with the wildest stories and anecdotes, and even the odd song. He was a natural entertainer, as many in the guesthouse trade were.

On the third day Auvonen announced, 'It's getting colder. Tomorrow we will start.'

'I have to go to Koirinoja first thing in the morning,' said our singing landlord. 'You could have a ride part of the way. Maybe we'll spot wolf tracks on the road.' We accepted his offer.

Having seen no sign of the wolf, ten kilometres south of Maisula we got out of the sleigh and began to ski slowly back: in the early morning light we might have missed something. After a few kilometres we met another sleigh. Its driver was coming from Loimola and knew Auvonen.

'What are you fellows up to? Your wolf crossed the road about two kilometres north of the guesthouse. The trail is as fresh as the scent of a young maiden. Some wolf hunters you pair are!' And with that he laughed and drove on.

We were soon at the spot where the wolf had crossed the road. He was heading west and within an hour we'd put him up. Our pursuit pace was considerably faster than anything I'd experienced with Korhonen. Indeed, Auvonen was the fastest ski runner I had ever known. His style wasn't particularly smooth but it was incredibly powerful and consumed great chunks of country.

We held this murderous pace for three days. On the fourth day it was becoming apparent that the wolf was tiring – and he wasn't the only one! I was so tired I was beginning to think I wouldn't see the hunt through. Suddenly Auvonen stopped. Leaning on his ski sticks he pointed at the trail. We were in our own tracks, tracks we had made just an hour earlier, tracks the wolf was now running in.

'He's running in circles and won't leave the hard-packed ski tracks again,' said Auvonen. 'You stay here and I'll follow the trail. If he doesn't show up in two hours then follow me. If he leaves the tracks then I'll drop a branch as a signal.' And with that, he was off again.

I checked the wind direction, found a fallen log and sat down, exhausted. The spot was a good one. I could see a hundred metres left and right, and our ski trail was about twenty-five metres away.

I blew the snow out of my gun's barrels, then opened my pack and pulled out a cooked grouse. I was starving. The bluish shadows of the spruce cast saw-tooth shapes on the snow, a woodpecker picked its way down a tree trunk, and a flock of snow buntings came by, the leading birds landing and the rear ones overtaking to land in front as they went on their way repeating this leap-frog manoeuvre over and over again.

I looked at my watch. Almost two hours had passed. Suddenly a shot rang out and I jumped to my feet. But no, the sound trailed on; it was just cracking ice. I began to breathe again. Then stopped! Not twenty metres away a large wolf loped along the trail.

It was too late to take careful aim. I raised the gun and fired. The wolf made a great leap and raced away. I fired again and it collapsed in the snow. I reloaded – dropping a cartridge in the process – and, still aiming, slowly approached the wolf; with the excitement I was prepared to ruin a good pelt with a close shot if I had to. Luckily he was stone dead. I flicked the safety catch back on and took a deep breath.

Auvonen now appeared, racing through the trees. He didn't stop until he saw the wolf. 'So, you did get him. When I heard the second shot I thought we'd lost him – usually the more shots fired the poorer the outcome.'

We made a big fire, had something to eat and rested. Then Auvonen skinned the wolf while I prepared our camp for the night.

'Well, by tomorrow afternoon we'll be in Maisula,' said Auvonen. 'I wonder how Korhonen will respond when he finds out we bagged the wolf in such a short time.'

'How will he find out, we're in the middle of nowhere?'

'Nowhere? We may not have telephones or a telegraph system and the mail may only come twice a week, but secrets are harder to keep here than in the city.'

Next morning we left for Maisula. Not long into our journey we crossed fresh wolverine tracks. 'How about we try and catch it?' I said. 'It's only got short legs.'

'You carry on but let me tell you, the faster you pursue him, the faster he will run – no matter how long the chase continues. The man who can tire a wolverine hasn't been born yet. Truly, the devil himself couldn't catch a wolverine.' I felt a little embarrassed at my ignorance and skied on in silence.

By afternoon we were sitting in the Maisula guesthouse. 'Here's a letter for you,' the landlady said waving it at me. 'It arrived today.' It was from St. Petersburg and had been sent to my Helsinki address. My mother had forwarded it to Uomais and the forester had sent it on. It was from Lisizin and written in German. After offering condolences about my father's passing he told me he would be travelling to the Urals to construct some smelters. The work would take about a month and he wondered if I might be interested in joining him. The smelters would only be about a hundred versts from Neratov's hunting lodge and I would be able to hunt with Gerasimov as much as I pleased. I quickly scribbled a note to the long-suffering forester Backman telling him of my new plans and also informing him that my brother would come and collect my eagle and dog. That I wouldn't be returning to my forestry career didn't require writing.

# 7
# Back to the Urals

Lisizin's letter had taken twelve days to get to me. Looking at the date of his planned departure, I knew I would only be able to make it if I left immediately. I ordered a sleigh for Kitelä and hoped there would be another available to take me on from there. I could send a telegram from Sortavala, travel to Helsinki and then take the evening train to St. Petersburg.

The journey to Kitelä was marked by an unfortunate incident. We hadn't been on the road long when there was a sudden rush of wings and a goshawk took a black grouse not twenty metres from us. The driver leapt from the sleigh, seized the grouse – the hawk having been frightened off – and handed it to me. And like an idiot, I took it. I didn't need it and now, late in the day, the hawk was unlikely to be successful again and would have to suffer the cold night without a meal. Even after all these years I still feel deep regret when I think of it.

That evening at the Kitelä guesthouse I enjoyed a good meal and turned in for the night. Sleep came quickly, but late in the night I was disturbed by tugging on my blanket. Still half asleep, I pulled back. The blanket thief pulled harder and I was soon involved in a proper tug of war! It turned out to be the landlady who needed the blanket because new guests had arrived!

I met these new guests the following morning, as I had to pass through their room to get to breakfast. They were two ladies of some standing who were sharing a bed. On seeing me they had hysterics and pulled the bedclothes over their heads. I was so very tempted to go and sit on the bed for a chat!

On to Sortavala, then Helsinki, where my arrival at the station aroused quite a bit of interest due to me still wearing my Lapp clothes! Half an hour later I was walking into my mother's house.

'Oh my God,' she cried. 'You look like a skeleton! Didn't they feed you out there in the wilderness?'

'He's probably just got TB,' said my brother reassuringly. 'Or maybe he died and they buried him on the mainland. This is just his ghost!'

Not surprisingly, my mother was worried about my trip out to the Urals, exclaiming, 'Son, son, all this can only end in unhappiness.' But I managed to calm her and reminded her that this would be my last chance to undertake a proper hunting trip for some time: my plan was to go to university in the autumn and study biology.

I met Lisizin at the main station in St. Petersburg and we travelled out like royalty – each with his own compartment. In Orsk our ways parted: he went northeast to work on the smelters; I went southeast. My sleigh driver, an elderly Russian who had spent many years in the army, told me that the winter had been a hard one. Hard enough in fact to drive packs of wolves into the villages; in some there wasn't a dog left, all had been taken by wolves. I listened eagerly, and he went on to entertain me throughout the journey. Some of his wolf stories were clearly fiction, and all of them fittingly gruesome. It was the typical hatred and fear always encountered in the more remote areas. Almost every guesthouse displayed a painting or two depicting the evil that wolves brought. Commonly a pack would be attacking a troika, the passengers defending themselves with guns while the driver whipped the horses on. More elaborate versions on this theme would have the wolves leaping up to tear the horses' throats out. One of the most imaginative I ever saw depicted a father throwing his children to the wolves as a distraction! Such paintings were as common in Russia as those of capercaillie in Finland.

As the sleigh pulled up at Neratov's hunting lodge Gerasimov came out to meet me. He ushered me inside, grabbed a bottle of vodka and deftly gave the bottom a hard blow with his right hand sending the cork towards the ceiling. He was clearly pleased to see me. We exchanged news, gradually coming to the planned wolf hunt. With the help of flag lines, a big drive had been arranged for the following day. Not only would I be able to attend, I was promised the chance of a shot. The thought of it all kept me awake most of the night.

Daybreak found us at the encircled wolf pack. Grouped around big fires, more than seventy hunt servants and beaters were waiting. More people were arriving in dribs and drabs and by the time the drive began we were well over a hundred strong. The flag lines encompassed an area of eight by four versts and had been set the evening before. During the night the wolves had been busy inspecting the lines but had not gone closer than about fifty paces – which was good. If a wolf gets too close to a flag line there's a chance he might not see it and wander through. Because of this it's vital that the flags are highly visible.

Those doing the shooting were positioned inside the cordoned off area and about fifty metres from the flag line. The plan was to press the wolves so they would run parallel to the flag line looking for a gap and run straight into the shooters. The key was not to push the wolves too hard – a requirement easily met as all the driving was to be done on foot through deep snow. Skis either weren't known or just not used by these local men.

In addition to guns, nets were also being employed. They were well over two metres high, olive and with mesh large enough for a wolf's head to pass through. Positioned wherever it was thought a wolf might run, they were hung so as to drop and envelop any wolf striking them, a spearman waiting about fifty metres away being ready to dispatch the captured animal. I asked Gerasimov if the nets were really necessary. After all it was clear we had plenty of shooters. 'You're right,' he said. 'There's no shortage of shooters these days. The main reason for their use is tradition. Netting simply belongs to wolf hunting. It's expected, like beating your wife on a Saturday night!' And he laughed loudly.

I'd been given what Gerasimov considered a good position but had been waiting for over an hour without seeing or hearing anything. Then to the left of me something moved. Gun ready, I looked along the flags, which hung limply as there wasn't a breath of wind. Had it been my imagination? I relaxed again and cradled the gun in my arms. Suddenly a wolf's head poked out of some nearby cover, the rest of its body slowly following. Then a second animal – and a third! They stared at the flags. They were so close together that a rifle could have killed two with one shot. I made a mental note to buy a drilling* as forester Backman had so often suggested.

Slowly the first wolf turned and disappeared into the bushes, followed by its companions. I carefully raised my gun again, expecting the wolves to reappear. They didn't, but a fresh one did, trotting along the flag line right at me! At about seventy metres he stopped and stared into the bushes. Could he sense the others? A few more steps and he was broadside to me. I was tempted to shoot but he was rather far, and a wolf has a tough hide. Before I could decide he'd vanished into the cover. I hardly dared breathe. Then he was back, coming out of the pines towards me. He was now about fifty metres – forty, thirty, twenty-five. I pulled the trigger. The shot threw him into the snow and he stayed down.

At that moment three wolves rushed past. I got a shot off at the first, but couldn't say if I'd hit him or not. I reloaded and rushed over to follow his tracks. About fifty metres along them I spied a few drops of blood. I'd hit him.

I returned to my position and held it until a sleigh came along some two hours later. A total of eight wolves had been shot. We loaded my wolf into the sleigh and I went off to follow the trail of the one I'd wounded, soon discovering that it had run into a net some eight hundred metres away and been finished off. I later discovered there were four pellets in its neck and another five in its lungs. That it had been able to run so far carrying that amount of damage demonstrates how tough the wolf is.

I took part in two more wolf drives over the next few days, but then

*A gun that combines two shotgun barrels with a single rifle barrel.

wolves became hard to find. After several days of waiting around, Gerasimov entered one evening and announced, 'I have a little job for you. There's a man living not far from here they call Ivan the Terrible. He's badly disfigured with a harelip and also has a cleft palate, which makes him sound like something from the animal kingdom. Before Christmas his horse died and he put its body behind the barn. He's already shot several foxes on it and last night he apparently saw a wolf eating from it. I told him you'd be happy to sit and watch the horse tonight in case the wolf returned. I thought it would suit you better than staring at four walls. A sleigh's already waiting.'

Gerasimov's description of Ivan was about right. The poor man was frightful to behold and his voice, if it could be called that, was like the snoring and murmuring of a bear. He'd once been married, but now, a widower, lived a lonely life in his dilapidated little house. He took me to the barn – which held two starving cows and some hens – and showed me a little low window through which I could watch the dead horse. I had a choice of seats: a milking stool or a sack stuffed with hay. The barn was about forty metres from the house and about a hundred metres from the edge of a wood.

I settled down to wait. The moon was high and I could see the whole snow-covered area between the barn and the edge of the woods. Time passed slowly. The cows were now asleep, just the occasional long sigh reminding me that they were there at all, and the hens had long since gone to roost.

Suddenly a fox! He was less than twenty paces away and checking the air in all directions. He'd come from around the corner of the barn, which is why I hadn't seen him sooner. I considered shooting him but decided against it: I wasn't going to lose my chance at a wolf for the sake of this fox.

The fox approached slowly, nose up, sniffing. Finally he relaxed and moved towards the horse, nose to the ground. Once he was convinced all was well, he lay down and began to gnaw at the frozen meat. It was hard work and he constantly changed position in an attempt to find an easier piece to work on. He stayed at the carcass for about two hours before heading back the same way he came. And that's all I saw the whole night.

At daybreak I woke Ivan. With some difficulty he communicated that we should have some tea. So as not to cause insult, I accepted his invitation even though I was offered a cup in which several cockroaches had met a sad end. My duty done, I asked him if he would drive me to the lodge. I would be back again that evening.

That night the fox returned and about half an hour later I detected something at the edge of the woods. The wolf, I thought and my heart began to pound like a drum. Carefully I followed every movement of the ghostly shadow as it eased, barely visible, along the woodland edge. He seemed to be in no hurry for a meal and remained an age in the darkness. I felt sure he had sensed the trap, but then suddenly he stepped fully into the moonlight – and became a fox!

After some snarling, he joined the first fox at the carcass, and with them eating from different ends, both stayed for several hours. Barely keeping awake, I kept watch all night, but no wolf – just daybreak and another cup of tea with Ivan!

# 8
# The Wolf Howler

My encounter with Ivan the Terrible was one of two little diversions while I waited for another wolf drive to be arranged. The second was a trip to The Wolf Howler!

This strange adventure presented itself during a conversation with Gerasimov about the reality of wolves attacking sleighs.

'I've been hunting wolves for years and never seen it. What I have seen is a wolf try and take a dog following a sleigh. Indeed, dogs are sometimes used as bait to lure a wolf close enough for a shot. I've even known piglets taken out in a sleigh in the hopes that their squeals will attract a wolf.'

He could see I was finding the whole thing hard to imagine and so continued, 'I know of a man who is supposed to be a master of the dog and sleigh hunt. He's a mysterious fellow, considered a shaman or wizard, and is feared for his reputation of having less visitors leave his remote lair than arrive! Locals call him The Wolf Howler. The moon is nearly full, if you feel bold enough what about us paying him a visit?' It was a challenge I couldn't resist.

As we headed north, the hills became higher and the forests darker as we made our way deeper into the Siberian wilderness. There were no roads, the only sign of human presence being the single sleigh trail that linked the widely spaced villages. Left and right the forest appeared endless and threatening, shadows and imagination giving our

Wolves being drawn within range by dragging a bag of pig dung behind the sleigh.

journey a supernatural feel.

Neither of us spoke. It was as if the stillness of the forest had cast a spell. Half asleep, Gerasimov let the horse choose its own speed. I envied his ability to doze. I felt decidedly uneasy with a weight on my chest as heavy as the snow burdening the forest that surrounded us. Had the shaman already woven me into some evil plan?

We stayed overnight with a Bashkir family – whose response to our destination did little to reassure me – and arrived at the wolf howler's hut around midday.

As we pulled up, a tall wild-eyed man stepped out. He had a long beard and was so thin he looked like he'd been dining on fresh air for a year. He slowly looked us over, stopped chewing his beard, and finally said, in a tenor voice that didn't fit the image at all, 'Well, you finally made it. I've been following your journey for hours.'

We didn't know quite how to react to this so Gerasimov simply began, 'This young gentleman has come to…' But the howler raised his hand.

'I know why he's come, he's here to hunt wolves with me. People like him carry a sign with them. You might not see it,' as he turned to Gerasimov, 'but I do, I see everything. There are no secrets from me. The boy has killed a werewolf, and it's going to follow him to his grave. See, there it is now!' And he pointed towards an open field, standing in which was a huge black wolf! We were stunned and just stood there staring at the wolf – which stared back. I turned to the sleigh and grabbed the first gun that came to hand, but I turned back to find the wolf gone. The howler let out a shrieking laugh. 'You were going to shoot it?' he hissed. 'Fool! How can you shoot a wolf that doesn't throw a shadow!'

Turning his back to us he began to take the harness off our horse. He then led it into the barn. As soon as he was out of sight, we raced to where the wolf had been standing. The snow was totally unbroken. No tracks!

As the three of us entered the cabin a large dog approached, growling. It took only a glance from its owner to have it scurry under the bed. I pulled out a bottle of vodka but to my surprise the howler turned it down. This was a new experience: he was the first person in the Urals I'd known reject a bottle of vodka.

We removed our furs and sat down on a little bench. The atmosphere was uncomfortable. The howler seemed to have forgotten us completely and aimlessly poked the fire. We sat in silence not knowing what to expect next. Finally he made some tea and motioned us to the table. The silence continued, broken only by the odd noisy slurp as the howler took a sip from his mug. Then suddenly he turned to me and said (actually he more sang it than said it), 'I could cure you of your urge to kill wolves. Stay here until autumn and you will go home cured.'

An already weird trip had just got very much weirder! Why did he have this strange notion I wanted to be 'cured'. I was quite happy with my wolf-hunting illness! And what was this about me staying there for months! What did he want with me! I thought carefully, the last thing I wanted was to trigger anger or possibly rage – and nothing would have surprised me from this wild-looking individual. Finally I said, 'I have met many great magicians' – which of course was nonsense – 'but none as great as you. If you can get a wolf to follow our sleigh tonight, I will consider your offer.' I put a ten-rouble bill on the table. 'As a sign of my admiration I ask you to accept this small gift.'

The bill disappeared into his pocket and he poured us some more tea. 'As soon as darkness comes we will leave. I will show you how to attract wolves, real wolves that have shadows – and leave tracks.' He'd obviously seen us looking for the werewolf's tracks.

Gerasimov got our provisions out of the sleigh and we settled down to a meal, inviting the howler to join us. He ate furiously, consuming half a cooked ham. Our vodka however he continued to decline.

After supper I went outside, going straight to the spot where the wolf had been standing. Scouring the ground, I went over the whole mysterious business again. At that time hypnosis – which I'm sure must have been at work – was not well known, which left me with only trickery or magic – or of course the howler's explanation.

Finally the day began to lean towards evening. My excitement was growing – what would happen out there in the night? But still we waited. The howler sat like a statue by the fire, elbows on knees, hands supporting his head. We didn't speak as conversation was something he clearly didn't want.

Eventually he rose, went to the barn and brought out a horse.

I was certainly glad to have Gerasimov with me. Alone it would have been a simple matter for this lunatic to dispose of me out there in the forest, killing me perhaps just for the cash I was carrying. Yes, he would have cured me alright, maybe with poison mushrooms, maybe a knife or noose!

'Don't worry,' Gerasimov whispered, as if he'd read my mind. 'If he brings a gun along I'll keep an eye on him.' And with that he pulled a revolver from his pocket. I had a shotgun with me in case I got a chance at a wolf, but if we got into trouble with the howler, Gerasimov's revolver would be much handier.

With the sleigh ready and both of us seated in the back, our host went into the house and returned with a double barrel shotgun. He climbed aboard, placing the gun in front of him, and we pulled away, his dog following at about twenty paces.

We took a trail leading north into the forest and pushed on for some time, the dog still following. At length the howler pulled the horse up, stood, and let out a howl so chilling it cut straight to my marrow. It truly wasn't human. Two more of these frightful howls followed, then he set the horse into a gallop. Gerasimov and I just looked at each other dumbfounded. After several hundred metres we stopped again – more howling, this time in a lower tone. We sat and waited while the howler scanned about, listening through the blackness. Then we were off again.

I glanced to Gerasimov, who had adjusted his position so that he could keep an eye on the howler. At the moment we were safe, but what if a wolf did appear and attack the dog? Then this creature up front had every right to stand and point his gun backwards. Gerasimov was stony faced; I knew he was ready for anything and almost certainly had his hand on his revolver.

Suddenly we came to a halt and could now hear a distant howl. It came twice then slowly tapered off.

Our man waited a couple of minutes, then let out a very low howl, followed by a much higher pitched one. We moved on again: more howling, all the time the pitch being altered to make it sound as if he were a whole pack of wolves.

A few minutes later he gave the dog some kind of sign and it began to bark furiously. Another sign, and the dog was quiet. Now the howler let out a sound reminiscent of a wounded dog; the reply from the wolves was instant – and it was near. The shaman urged the horse on, all the while making barking sounds. At the shoreline of a lake he stopped and went into a true barking frenzy, before driving out onto the ice, following the shoreline.

The howler raised his hand and the dog fell back, following us now at about a hundred metres. Three wolves rushed out of the trees, heading for the dog, which was now racing for its life towards the sleigh. Two of the wolves stopped, but the third raced on after the dog. At thirty paces I let it have a full load straight in the chest. Its tail went up, the front feet collapsed and it slid along the hard snow and was still.

The howler hadn't touched his gun.

Gerasimov, not prone to outbursts of excitement, let fly with praise, commenting on the 'pure genius' of tempting the wolf into the open on the ice. The howler stayed calm. He slowly climbed from the sleigh, went over to the wolf and dragged it back to us by its front feet. 'An old female,' he said and placed the wolf behind his seat. Then he took the shells out of his gun and turned to Gerasimov. 'Now you can put your revolver away.'

# 9
# The Bear Hunt

Back at the lodge Gerasimov was handed a letter. It was from Lisizin. Wolf hunting was to take a backseat: Neratov had invited two counts of the family Dolgoruki to a bear hunt at the lodge. Gerasimov was to let Neratov know the moment the local bears had woken from hibernation and to ensure that at least two were flagged in. As Neratov himself wasn't sure he would be able to join the hunt, Lisizin would play host. He would be at the lodge as soon as possible.

Gerasimov was clearly concerned, and it was indeed a heavy responsibility. As soon as the bears emerged from their winter dens, the mating season began. This made them restless wanderers, and the males in particular were constantly on the move. Under these conditions it would take a lot of luck to flag any in and Gerasimov knew how impatient visiting dignitaries could be: these counts probably expected a quick sleigh ride in to the woods to take their pick of bears!

In an effort to locate the required bears, Gerasimov and I spent several days travelling from village to village, talking to hunters, government officials and preachers. The latter were particularly important because they could deliver our mission to their congregations – and relay the rewards: twenty roubles for every reported bear track, and if the bear could be flagged in – a hundred roubles! Preacher, official or hunter, to make sure our message got spread, all were bribed with gifts of vodka.

It didn't take long for the first report to come in: some distance away the tracks of three bears had been spotted. Gerasimov gambled the report was accurate and sent Neratov a telegram: his guests should come as soon as possible, the weather had warmed and there was a danger the snow would thaw which would make finding the bears extremely difficult.

Three days later Lisizin arrived. He was tense, and his mood spread like fire through the lodge as the place was meticulously prepared for the guests. It was no small task. The bear hunt had not been planned and the lodge had been badly neglected since its last guests several months earlier.

Updates on the bears arrived daily. They were being tracked by reliable hunters and holding to a specific area. With the snow still deep, things looked good.

It was about now that Lisizin confessed a slight concern. How was he to explain my presence at the lodge to the counts, who would surely wonder what this young Finnish-born German was doing there. I could see his point and suggested I play the role of one of Neratov's hunt servants. He protested at first, but not very strongly, and seemed quite relieved when I later appeared in my white fur coat and black fur hat.

Gerasimov and I now set off to make the final arrangements for the hunt. The bears were off to the northeast and up in the mountains. This is where we needed to be. We stopped to rest with the Bashkir family from our howler trip, got a fresh horse and continued on. As we travelled, Gerasimov established a courier service that had riders exchanging messages between the various villages. It was a costly business but Gerasimov could be very free with cash when the need arose.

After what felt like an endlessly long trip, we arrived at a tiny village consisting of just a few huts. We were met by a tracker who informed us that the bears were spending their time along an open brook. In his opinion they could now be flagged in. But Gerasimov wasn't sure: the counts probably hadn't yet arrived at the lodge, and even if they had, it would take them at least two days to get to us – possibly longer with the pampered way they would be accustomed to travelling. The bears would not stay within the flags for more than two

days even if the area involved was massive, and once they had broken out, they wouldn't hesitate to do so again. That evening however, a courier arrived with a message: the counts would be arriving at the lodge tomorrow. As the letter had been three days getting to us, we could probably expect our guests in the morning, the day after at the latest. Gerasimov thought for a moment then ordered the bears to be flagged in early the next day.

The owls were still hooting when we set off next morning. It was quite a convoy. The first sleigh carried four local hunters, the second, two more. Gerasimov and I occupied sleigh number three and behind us were four more sleighs with flag lines and men.

On arrival, two hunters were sent to check that the bears were still in the area to be encircled. They were back in two hours having seen no tracks to indicate otherwise, and a few hours later the flag lines were hung.

Gerasimov and I returned to the village to receive Lisizin and the counts: if they arrived early the hunt could take place immediately. We'd hardly settled ourselves when their sleighs came racing into the village. They had travelled in single horse affairs, the narrow roads not

permitting the troikas normally used for guests. But a degree of pomp had been maintained: each man – Lisizin included – occupied his own sleigh.

While Gerasimov was delivering his report, I stayed in the background. Lisizin gave a quick nod in my direction, but didn't openly acknowledge me.

I studied the two counts. One was a big man with piercing blue eyes; the other was smaller with blue-black hair and almost black eyes. Both were in their thirties and carried themselves poorly – there was certainly not the slightest hint of any military background. Nor did anything about them hint at any kind of involvement in hunting or indeed any outdoor activity. But perhaps I'd be proved wrong.

It was decided to immediately proceed with the hunt and we set off for the flagged bears. We arrived to find the wind coming from the west, so those doing the shooting – the counts could not cover the whole area alone – didn't have to travel far to their positions. The counts were placed in the middle, Lisizin off to the left, while I was on the right flank. I was armed with a 32-calibre Winchester Special. It was the quickest repeating rifle I owned. I'd brought it to the Urals thinking it might come in handy – and that's just how it felt for this bear hunt. Unfortunately its unusual nature drew the dark count's attention. 'Where did you get this?' he said snatching it from me.

'I bought it.'

'Where?'

'In Reval,' I lied.

'Where are you from? You're certainly not Russian.'

'Estonia, Your Grace.'

'So, you probably speak German?'

'Yes.'

Now he spoke in German. 'You're not Estonian. Why are you lying? Maybe you're related to some Baltic baron?'

'No Your Grace, my father was German but no baron. My mother is Swedish.'

He gave me my gun back. 'Well, maybe,' he said, but he didn't sound satisfied.

'How do you pronounce the name of the ship Retvizan, and what does it mean?'

'Rettvisan,' I said, 'and it means honesty.'

'Good,' he said. 'Now tell me how you come to be here?'

Lisizin, who had been looking increasingly nervous throughout all this, now came to my aid. 'Neratov knows the lad Your Grace. He's here at his invitation.' Finally he seemed satisfied and complimented himself on his powers of observation – nobody could pull the wool over his eyes.

I knew the drive would be well underway and was glad to be rid of the nosy fellow. The area to be driven was not very large and would take about two hours to work through. However, in less than half that time loud cursing came down the line. It was Gerasimov. I could only imagine that the bears had broken through the flags.

I was still with this thought when the nosy count came over. I was right about his lack of hunting experience: a seasoned hunter would have stayed at his post until the end of the drive.

'What's happening?' he said loudly, while still some thirty paces away. Rather boldly, I held my finger to my lips and whispered that I suspected the bears had broken through the flags. I wanted to send him back to his post, but knew this would take things too far and so suffered his company as he continued to chat, ignoring my clearly agitated face.

Finally, Gerasimov appeared. 'Through the flags?' I inquired. He nodded, but I could tell that wasn't the whole story.

It was decided that Lisizin would take the two counts into the village where accommodation had been arranged. With them comfortable, an effort would be made to flag the bears back in – a move I found extremely optimistic. And even if we did manage to flag them in, having crossed the line once, they'd never stay put.

As it turned out, the story of the bears going through the flags was pure fiction – a tale to save the embarrassment of having the counts know there'd been no bears within the flagged area to begin with! Gerasimov was furious. 'I should have become a monk and saved myself the misery of working with such morons.' He'd noticed the bears' tracks along the brook during the drive, noticing too that they'd followed the trickle of water to end up way outside the area that had been flagged in. He turned to the men gathered around us. 'Don't just stand there like idiots. Get the flag lines down! Tomorrow those bears MUST BE FLAGGED IN! Do you understand – BEARS FLAGGED IN, not just a pretty bit of forest!' The hunters didn't move. 'What are you waiting for! GO!'

Next morning the bears were indeed flagged in, and by noon the beaters were at work and we were in position and waiting. About an hour had passed when the forest suddenly gave up the most terrible screaming. It was pure horrible agony. I rushed for the trees, pushing the dark count – who for some reason was running towards me – to one side, telling him to remain there.

Into the forest and I was soon confronted with a beater shrieking wildly as he ran from tree to tree desperately trying to stay ahead of a huge bear. His battle was soon lost. The bear grabbed him, tossed him into the snow like a puppet, and with him face down, began furiously biting at his hips and buttocks. The screaming was unbearable and the snow, red with blood. I ran to the man's aid but didn't dare to shoot until I was within a few strides. I then raised my gun, aimed right for the bear's head and squeezed the trigger – and nothing happened! I pulled another cartridge into the chamber and tried again. Still nothing! I was now panicking and on the verge of clubbing the bear with the rifle butt when Gerasimov rushed over and killed the bear with a single shot. I later discovered that the firing pin in my rifle was broken.

The beater was in a terrible state and while Gerasimov and I tried to prevent him bleeding to death two men went for a sleigh. They were soon back, bringing numerous other people, including Lisizin and the two counts. A first aid kit was produced – it was something the dark count never travelled without – and the injured man was attended to as best we could under the circumstances: at least he was now stable enough to transport to the village. Before the sleigh moved off, the

dark count discretely tucked an undisclosed sum of money into the man's coat pocket. He seemed genuinely concerned.

Later I learned that the two counts had in fact managed to shoot their bears. During my rush into the forest I'd heard shots and these were now explained, as was the rage the bear had displayed towards the beater. The trackers had been following a female with two – now dead – two-year-old cubs.

That evening we had news that the injured man was set to make a full recovery, and with the counts having gone home happily clutching their bear skins, we celebrated in fine style. We drank to the health of the Tsar, to Neratov and to the Wolf Howler. We drank to brotherhood and friendship that even death couldn't conquer, and finally we drank to the fair maidens our wine and food had attracted, maidens whose soft arms bid warm welcome when tiredness finally overcame us.

Next day, Lisizin and I packed for the journey home. It was a pleas-

ant trip and we talked of all that had happened. But as we parted in St. Petersburg his face was suddenly full of concern. 'Your father was a good friend to me and I worry for your future. I see troubled times ahead and urge you to take Finnish citizenship.' More he wouldn't say. I never saw him again.

# 10
# The Duck Hunters

It was 1908 and the swifts were circling the towers of the Nikolai Church in Helsinki. I'd been waiting for their calls, scanning the skies on my way to the university, hoping they would soon arrive. Now they were here! They were heralds, their calls those of promise. In a few days, migrating ducks would appear out at sea in flocks hundreds of thousand strong. For a duck hunter it was the year's highlight.

None of these migrating ducks ventured inland. Instead they followed the coastline, clinging to its many islands. A little west of Helsinki and far out at sea, there were three such islands always very popular with duck hunters. They were about one and a half kilometres apart, so small as to be little more than rocks, and all of granite worn conspicuously smooth by ice. The largest of them was Österbådan, which lay to the east and was about four metres high at its highest point. Then followed Sankbådan, a totally smooth little island that didn't protrude much more than a metre above the sea. Furthest to the west lay Westerbådan, about fifty metres long, ten wide and at its easterly end about two and a half metres high. For duck hunting, Westerbådan was always the best because the quarry arrived from the west.

Sankbådan was only safe in calm weather. If the wind came up you had to leave immediately because as the waves grew it became impossible to launch the boat. With you trapped, the waves would now wash right over the rock taking you with them! Österbådan was quite different. Here even an overnight stay wasn't considered risky. Westerbådan lay somewhere between the two. It was generally safe, but certain winds could make it lethal, the most dangerous being those from the southwest. When these blew in, odd conditions were created that brought a very real danger of you being swept away. Three fishermen had suffered this fate many years ago: their names had been chiselled into the granite, with a verse warning that the rock should be abandoned if a storm approached.

At that time I had a special boat called an ekstock ('oak log'), a traditional vessel that would have once been hewn from a single oak, hence the name. It was about seven metres long, open, and had a keel that could be raised. It was also fitted out with yacht tackle that could be taken down in a hurry. There was no motor at all. Boat motors were still in their infancy and were heavy and unreliable. The rich used them, but then they weren't proper sailors. For most of us, getting about the islands involved the traditional skills of rowing and sailing.

In readiness for the first duck sortie, I'd prepared the boat some weeks earlier: the hull had been coated with tar and the rigging and ropes checked and renewed where necessary. Going with me would be two university friends: one would eventually become a colonel in the Finnish army, the other a doctor.

We set sail for Westerbådan five days after the swifts' arrival. It was a tense time. An unwritten law forbad landing on the rock if it had already been claimed by other shooters. Would it still be available? We were a little more than a kilometre from the island when we spotted a boat. She was heading straight for Westerbådan and would probably get there first. Just as if someone had sounded an alarm, one of my companions joined me at the oars and we began rowing for all we were worth. Crew member number three manned the tiller. We worked like machines for about half an hour before the other boat finally admitted defeat and set course for Sankbådan. We arrived at Westerbådan to find it free.

Even in calm weather, landing on the island was tricky due to its metre-wide perimeter coating of slippery green slime. To avoid landing on this and sliding into the sea you had to make a huge leap from the bow. With all of us having achieved this, the boat was heaved up onto the rock a little so that we could unload our provisions, ammunition and cooking gear. Once the boat was empty, the tackle came down. The main sail was thrown over the provisions basket and drinking water and kept in place with the mast. This little stash, on the south side of the rock, would also act as a shooting blind.

My two friends now rowed out some twenty metres and anchored the decoys in front of the blind. In the meantime I drenched the sail with water to darken it. This way it would blend better with the granite. Our preparations made, the boat was hauled fully out so that it wouldn't break the silhouette of the rock and we sat down behind the blind and waited.

The sun rose on the northeastern horizon; the air was warm and clear and the wind had died right down. It was a perfect May morning. In the far west we could hear the melodic calls of long-tailed ducks looking for mussels, 'Ali, ali, ali,' their song in its different tones and colours ringing out a symphony of nature.

Further south, huge 'curtains' of the birds flew by – a big moving curtain being exactly what they looked like. Such ducks wouldn't come to the decoys, but smaller groups of perhaps ten or fifteen were often fooled. These were always shot on the wing – more sporting than waiting for them to settle on the water – and were generally attempted as soon as they were within range. The bagged ducks weren't collected until we'd finished shooting, which would be around nine in the morning with the final flights. Then it was time to get the gas burner out and prepare breakfast. During the day we would often just watch the migrating birds. An enormous variety would pass by and as a biology student I usually sat all day with binoculars making notes. Twice I shot waders that had never before been observed in Finland.

That first morning we shot twenty birds, about average when the migration was in full swing and the weather was good. Under poor conditions the count might be zero.

The following morning the decoys were out before light, but it wasn't long before our thoughts turned to the cloudy sky and the

southwest wind that was swiftly building. We hurriedly brought the decoys back in and pulled the boat higher onto the rock. None of us thought of leaving, despite the granite-chiselled warning.

By noon the southwest wind had turned into a southwest storm, and leaving the island was impossible: the sea was now a foaming maelstrom, the wind blowing the foam off the tops of the waves with such force that the whole island was being covered.

It was time for swift action. We dug out our waterproof gear and moved the boat again, dragging it to the highest possible location and anchoring it as best we could by driving one point of the anchor into a crack in the rock. We then laid the mast on top of it from bow to stern, threw all our kit into it and covered the whole boat with the main sail, tying it down securely. We then crawled inside and made ourselves as comfortable as possible.

The plan was for two of us to sleep while the other stood a four-hour watch. At the end of my watch on the first evening, I looked out to discover that the island had lost at least a third of its size. I scanned across the vastness of the black and white sea and watched a wild confusion of waves chasing and consuming each other as they raced towards us.

We seemed set to be washed like toys from our little rock. But we had an ally. A hundred metres out was a reef and as the walls of raging waves hit this, they were violently burst to come crashing at us with much less power. Without this reef, we'd have been gone already. But how long before the sea was whipped up into a force that even this couldn't save us from? Even now the breaking water was periodically lifting the boat. I looked over to Sankbådan and Österbådan. They were gone. Not even the larger islands to the far north were visible. We were alone, our little boat a sad coffin covered with a grey shroud.

Early next morning the roar of the waves was interrupted by a ship's horn and we peered out to find a vessel from the Helsinki coast guard. She was some way off but through our binoculars we could see the crew urging us to make our way over to them. It would have been suicide: our boat would have been smashed into a thousand pieces on the rock. Like it or not we were prisoners, stuck until the weather changed – or fate decided a less happy ending.

Using hand signals we tried to tell the ship we were staying put and they were to steam back to Helsinki. Eventually they got the message and left.

On the mainland we now became famous as the local paper swooped on our story, headlines telling how we had shunned help and were just waiting for the weather to break so that we could continue hunting! It's surprising what can be read from a few hand signals!

After three days – the inhabitants of Helsinki having received daily news updates – the storm abated and, as insane as it sounds, we did exactly what the paper had said we would – we continued hunting!

Immediately we discovered that the storm had worked in our favour: it had broken up the big flocks, leaving small numbers to be repeatedly drawn to the decoys. On that first morning we shot – and it's something I'm still ashamed of – over eighty ducks, and only stopped then because we were out of ammunition. And still it wasn't enough: two of us made a trip to the mainland to get more cartridges.

On the following day it was clear that the ducks had regrouped, with only a few coming to the decoys. In the afternoon we sat on the highest point of the rock and watched spellbound as the curtains flew by. It was simply unimaginable. They continued hour after hour without interruption. We attempted to count the birds they contained by dividing the curtains into squares and counting the number in each square. The result was two hundred thousand birds per hour! While the accuracy of this count is of course extremely questionable, it still paints a movement of staggering proportions.

We remained on the rock for another two days, but didn't shoot much. Our total bag for the hunt was a hundred and thirty six.

A week after our return to Helsinki we sailed out again, this time equipped with boring chisels, hammers and three strong iron rings. We fixed one ring close to the shore, for tying up in good weather, and the two others, one for each end of the boat, at the spot where we had made our emergency camp. We also chiselled our names and the date into the granite.

Sixty-five years later I received a letter from one of my old comrades – the colonel. With his note were a few photos of Westerbådan, including one showing our long-ago chiselled names. Apparently, the daughter of the now long-dead doctor had been out to the rock and come across them quite by chance. She had tracked down the colonel to tell her story.

# 11
# Times of Change

In 1910 I became engaged, marrying in May 1911. After the wedding, my young wife* and I took the duck-hunting boat to my old home district on the north shore of Lake Ladoga. I'd been employed to study the lake's bird life and we sailed from island to island spending most nights under the stars. From a scientific point of view the study wasn't too successful, and in all honesty not carried out too thoroughly. But I did notice one strange thing: long-tailed ducks, which I'd always associated with the open sea, were here and mixing with puddle ducks like mallards. However they didn't stay long: they left for Lapland and the Kola Peninsula to raise their broods on the small tundra lakes.

The lake project completed, that autumn we moved to Germany where I continued my studies in Munich and Kiel.

In 1914 war broke out and, wearing the German uniform, I was sent to the Eastern Front, first to East Prussia, later to the Carpathians where things were getting pretty serious. I was wounded in the Carpathians and after spending time in several hospitals in Austria, finally ended up in a military hospital in Kiel.

After my release I was ordered to Sweden. Recruits from Finland were being formed into the 27th Jäger Battalion and moved through Sweden into Germany. With my language skills I was an ideal instruc-

*Impi Sandberg. She ran dancing classes, which is where she met Remmler.

tor-translator, as was my brother, who was also involved. We spent time in Stockholm, Malmö, Haparanda and Umeå.

I eventually returned to Kiel and was transferred to a naval battalion – which soon saw me back in Sweden (Umeå) assisting in the delivery of weapons to Finland. My main occupation however was sabotage. A winter road – running partly on a frozen river – was being used to transport arms and ammunition from America to the Russian army. The shipments were moved by horse-drawn sleigh and thousands of sleighs toiled day and night at the task. Germany of course made every effort to stop this leak in the blockade and the road became one of the main goals of my sabotage activities. I immediately targeted the sleigh horses: they were infected with glanders bacillin and died in their hundreds. A further tactic focused on the ammunition boxes. These were opened and the odd explosive cartridge inserted into the machine gun belts – which blew up the gun as well as its operator. They were desperate days.

The end of the war found me in Finland. Rather aimlessly, I followed some friends to Maxmo, a small fishing community consisting mostly of islands near Vaasa in the Narrows of Quarken. The people of this archipelago lived a life frozen in time, their methods and ways already a century behind those of the mainland. They farmed as their great grandfathers had and spoke a Swedish dialect that, caught in passing, sounded almost like English. It was unique to the area. The daring, reliability and proud nature of these islanders made them the truest company you could wish for – but only if you were of similar ilk. They openly despised the slovenly and slack mettled.

With the eagle owls having barely laid their first eggs, the local hunters were getting ready for the annual seal hunt. There were two species of seal in the Bay of Bothnia. The most common was the small ring seal. This animal doesn't give birth on the ice like other seals, but hollows out a snowdrift so that the pup can remain hidden until it loses its white coat and can enter the sea. Before this, such pups are extremely vulnerable. The fishermen of Hogland Island kept dogs that were specially trained to sniff them out, the white coat, which turns yellowish during the tanning process, being a valuable pelt.

The other seal in the Bay of Bothnia was the larger grey seal. Unlike the ring seal, this animal couldn't bore holes in the ice and so for safety had to rely on the open water between the ice floes. This dependency could result in trouble. In very cold calm weather it was possible for the water between the floes to freeze so thick that the seals couldn't break it. If this happened they would panic and begin wandering in a straight line, usually heading south. Once on this course nothing would sway them and they would continue over great lumps and chunks of broken ice, even when a minor detour offered a much easier passage. Usually this stubbornness would eventually lead them to open water and salvation. But not always. A fisherman once told me that his wife went out to milk the cows and found three seals against the barn wall. They had come across the island and, unwilling to go around the barn, could now go no further. It was a nice find for the farmer, but, quite literally, the end of the road for the seals.

In those days a seal hunter's equipment consisted of a large open sailboat, and one, sometimes two, smaller boats, these having runners so that they could be dragged with ease on the ice. Once the drift ice was reached the main boat would be hauled out and used as living quarters for the crew. The smaller boat or boats were then used for forays out across the ice floes, which might extend to several square kilometres. Where sections of open water were met, the boats were simply used as intended then hauled out again onto the next solid floe. Operating this way, great distances could be covered in a day.

When a seal was sighted, one man would stay with the boat while the other would head towards the quarry on an oversized, brass-bottomed ski called a stang: standing on one foot he would kick himself along with the other, reaching incredible speeds on smooth ice. When he got to a point where there was a risk of being spotted by the seal, he would lie down on the stang and propel himself forwards with his hands. On the front of the stang there was a small rectangular cloth shield with a slit in it for the rifle, which was usually ex-Swedish army. Most shots were taken at not much more than a hundred metres. Above this, fine accuracy couldn't be guaranteed, and for success the seal had to receive a brain shot. If the brain wasn't hit, the seal would dive into its escape hole (or if a grey seal the open sea), no matter how much damage the bullet had done.

Because of this need for accuracy, no one unable to hit a matchbox at a hundred metres would ever be taken on as crew. Telescopic scopes being unknown to these people, each seal hunter designed his own sighting device. Often these homemade sights were so fine that those not familiar with them couldn't hit a thing. Sometimes the setup was unnecessarily complicated, the same accuracy being achievable with a much easier to use arrangement. But to suggest such a thing would have been a complete waste of time: these seal hunters were the most conservative people on earth.

Having often discussed seal hunting with northern fishermen, I decided to join a seal boat and ended up crewing with two young men under an elderly captain. Our skipper had been a fisherman since boyhood. It had clearly been a life of much toil and little reward. His humble dwelling stood on bare rock, the only area suitable for cultivation being a small patch of soil in a bit of a depression. This is where he grew his potatoes. The crop produced was small, but a widower now living alone, it was sufficient. Like most of his kind he knew only one type of food: a pot full of potatoes with a thick layer of fresh or salted fish on top. Should a duck or a grouse come his way, this would replace the fish as way of variety.

The old man had agreed to take me along purely as a guest – and one that, he quipped, 'hopefully didn't have too big an appetite!' There would be no pay and certainly no share of the profits. He was of course highly sceptical about my guns, and viewed my German Sports Mauser with great distrust. I was eventually able to win him over with my Stecher, but only after I had hit a small Finnish ten-penny piece five times in a row, shooting prone.

So, one morning, a stiff south wind having broken the ice from the island and driven it northwards, we set sail from Björkö. Around noon we reached the drift ice and were forced to work our way into the main pack, rowing and pulling. Finally, at the main floe we hauled the boat out onto the ice, covered it with the sails and secured everything. Our camp was ready.

As we only had one smaller boat with us, it was decided that two of us should use stangs to explore the nearer ice floes while the others took the boat westwards on a longer excursion.

Because the use of a stang was completely new to me, I was keen to experiment and set off on my own. I'd hardly been underway half an hour when I spotted a seal through the binoculars. The distance was about a kilometre. As it was lying in the sun, I didn't head straight for it but kept a little to the left. About half a kilometre away from it I stopped and got down on the ski, swung a little to the right and started to crawl towards it. Having had the 'one hundred metres rule' fully drummed into me, I eased carefully to within range, got the rifle in position and waited until my breathing was back to normal. I aimed very carefully, and fired. At the shot, the animal's head dropped and stayed down. Success! I'd stalked my first seal.

But now I had a little problem. What to do with it? My fellow crew members had obviously assumed I was familiar with the routine and so neglected this part of my education. I went over my options. To drag the whole seal back to camp probably wasn't the right thing to do. I knew the fat and hide were important – and the skull. The latter was valuable because the state – Finland and Sweden – paid a premium for every lower jaw. At one time Sweden paid for the front flippers, but hunters soon exploited the flaw in this: Swedish hunters would meet with their Finnish opposites out on the ice and exchange items; the Finns would give the Swedes the flippers while the Swedes would give the Finns the lower jawbone. It wasn't long before the authorities got wise to it.

I thought for a minute then played safe: I placed the whole thing on the ski and dragged it back to camp. As predicted this was not how things were done. The skilled seal hunter would skin the kill, leaving the fat on the pelt, and, discarding the body, keep only the head.

With the shooting of that first seal came another new experience – eating it. That night one of my companions took some of the very dark meat and prepared our evening meal. Although during the war my brother and I had regularly purchased seal meat for the German government, I had never tasted it and approached my plate with trepidation. I was pleasantly surprised. True it wasn't the tastiest stew I'd ever tried, but I'd eaten a lot worse. And the meat was very lean: a seal's body might be covered with a thick layer of fat but the meat itself is not at all fatty.

Despite a hearty meal I didn't sleep well. Two members of the crew had brought seal pups back to camp, the little white infants having been simply clubbed to death. I knew this was part and parcel of seal hunting but now, facing possible involvement, it turned my stomach. It was something I would take no part in. But how to get out of it?

Next morning I declared that I wanted to go out on my own again. It was actually my turn with the boat but I argued that I needed practice with the stang.

All day I searched the floe, climbing every mound to check the area with my binoculars, but there was nothing but ice and snow. Finally, as the day neared its end and I'd begun my trek home, I got a sighting. I came over a great barrier of ice and there, not fifty metres away, was a seal. It was there for about two seconds: as soon as it saw me it went into its hole. I checked the wind, found a good spot near the hole, and sat for about an hour. But luck wasn't with me – the seal didn't return.

I arrived back at camp to find the others already eating. None of them had seen a thing all day.

The following day my attempts to go out alone failed miserably and I was partnered with the old man and the boat. Having seen no seals, we eventually arrived at the northwest edge of our ice floe. The next floe was about forty metres away. How big this floe was couldn't be ascertained, but looking across it there was no sign of open water. We crossed the gap and continued on. Ten minutes later we stopped and set up a flag; this would act as something to home in on. We then separated, leaving the boat to set off on our stangs. My companion went inland; I stayed closer to the edge of the floe.

In the afternoon I finally spotted a seal, but she had a little white-coated pup with her. What was I to do? My duty was to shoot the seal and club her baby. That's why I was here. But I couldn't do it.

I moved inland, soon spying the old man in the far distance. He appeared to be heading back to the boat, heavily laden. I slid towards him; he'd shot two seals and clubbed two white pups. 'Haven't you seen anything?' he asked, looking at me rather suspiciously. I got the distinct feeling he somehow sensed my guilt.

Next morning my three companions took off with the small boat while, at my own request, I stayed to hunt nearer our base. So it went for the next two weeks. The hunting was good and the pile of hides next to the camp boat grew steadily higher. However, my own contribution to this pile lacked one very obvious element – I killed not a single white pup. No one commented on this but one day the old man came over and quietly said, 'I don't like killing the pups either.'

One day it rained all afternoon, and in the evening, when the weather turned colder, we had what the Americans call 'freezing rain'. This coated everything in a thick layer of ice and made it lethal underfoot. Indeed, if we hadn't been equipped with wide footwear made of sealskin, it would have been impossible to stand, let alone walk. The soles to these shoes were the key: made from un-tanned cowhide, they gripped well.

After much discussion it was decided that the old man and I would remain on the home floe, while the others would take the boat.

'Pay attention,' my companion said soberly as we separated. 'Get back to camp immediately if a wind comes up. You won't be able to walk against it on this surface.'

I set off in a southwesterly direction, the stang flying across the slippery ice with almost dangerous velocity.

Despite the ground I was covering, the terrain seemed devoid of life. Then through the binoculars I spotted a grey seal, easy to distinguish from a ring seal due to the high-held head and raised rear flippers, a habit typical of its kind when out on the ice.

When I got to within about eight hundred metres I could see she was at the edge of a vast area of open water. I lay down on the stang and crawled towards her. It was windstill and so there was no danger of her getting my scent. At about a hundred and fifty metres I stopped. Grey seals tend to be very alert; I didn't dare go closer. I took my time – even setting the gun down a couple of times because I wasn't steady enough – and when the crosshairs of my scope were exactly on the seal's skull, I fired. She dropped, remained motionless, and I made my way to her.

Now the less pleasant part – skinning. It was hard work and tough on the back: this was a big animal with a layer of fat under the skin nearly five centimetres thick. I straightened up a few times – at one point I even sat on the carcass and lit my pipe. Because the seal's head was so large and badly damaged from the shot, I kept only the lower jawbone, stuffing it inside the hide at the front of the stang.

So occupied had I been, I'd failed to notice something of dire importance. Legend has it that in the magic lands of the high north – the lands of ghosts and spirits – a dragon was born. He grew quickly and, having not sufficient room in the mountains, spread his vast wings and flew south, eventually reaching the Quarken Narrows. Here he was halted by the sun to remain forever, a fearless guardian.

That this guardian was about to unleash an ice hell would have been clear to any living creature – except me. Busy with my seal, I'd been oblivious to what was brewing behind me. That is until little shards of ice came whispering past my feet. I turned and the dragon was on me. Huge streams of ice crystals hit me as the wind, now whistling and whining, blew in so hard it dragged the skinned seal into the sea, and would have taken the stang and my gun if I hadn't moved quickly enough. I grabbed them and struggled away from the water, deeper onto the ice, snow now coming at me so thick I couldn't see a thing. Suddenly, a sledgehammer gust of wind hit me in the chest. It was so strong it would have blown me away if I hadn't thrown myself to the ground. With the stang and gun now crossways under me and wedged against two chunks of ice, I hung on for all I was worth. It was impossible to see: I couldn't even open my eyes.

Luckily my mittens were tied to a strap. Had they been lost I'd never have held on. My white sailcloth parka was also an asset. Worn over my furs, its hood could be pulled over my headgear and done up to stop the snow getting down my neck.

Very carefully I raised the stang enough so that I could clamp it under my arm. This done, I felt more secure but in half an hour the arm felt dead and useless. Continually switching arms I struggled on: I could cope with the pain just as long as the stang stayed in place.

I've spent many unpleasant nights in the open, but this one remains in a class of its own. My main worry was how long – stuck in one position – I could endure the torture of the cold. To even attempt to seek more shelter would have been suicide: I'd have been swept into the sea. The storm was coming from the north, so I knew it was going to get colder. I also knew that these storms could last two days. Could I hang on that long? Would I even get the chance: what if the floe broke up!

Time crawled and I prayed for daylight so that I could better assess my situation: maybe there was some kind of protection nearby. But daylight didn't come, and the storm didn't abate. The whole thing seemed unreal, me out here clinging to a piece of ice while far away in the normal world, people were tucked up snug in their beds. Why hadn't I been more careful.

Suddenly there was a mighty vibration through the ice. I held my breath, terrified that the floe was breaking up. But no, a few more shakes and bumps and all was still. The snow was now partially covering me – a drift having formed against me – and all the while the howling of the wind continued, now stronger than ever. I strained hard, listening for the one thing I feared above everything – the sound of surf. My floe was so large that there seemed no danger of the sea being able to destroy it, but under these conditions anything seemed possible.

One thing was absolutely sure: the storm and the snow were no longer coming at me head on. Had the wind changed or had the floe turned? I assumed the latter and my mind ran wild: I was now being swept down the Finnish coast and the bumps I was feeling were from collisions with islands or where the floe was gliding over reefs. I was going to end up in some giant ice pile and be crushed as if by mortar and pestle. Or maybe I'd be simply swept out into the open sea never to be seen again.

I tried to move a little and found to my great surprise that I was stuck fast. The little snowdrift that had been collecting about me now held me tight. Paradoxically, this seemingly distressing situation actually came to my aid: kept in place by the snow, I didn't need to hang on to the stang, and the snow actually warmed me. Not much could happen to me as long as the floe survived. Sooner or later the weather would have to settle.

At some point I must have fallen asleep. I was back in the war and frantically trying to free myself from a tangle of barbed wire. My wife was there, wandering towards me across the battlefield and whispering of happier times to come, of life on the island where the falcons nested and of the family we would raise. I struggled still harder and was suddenly awake: I was out of my snow mound and facing a bright day.

A strong wind still swept over the ice but the hurricane-like force of the previous day had gone. I looked about for a landmark. I should have been able to see the lighthouse on Valsörarna but it just wasn't there, nor indeed was any land at all.

My compass soon relayed that what had been north, was now west. Just how many times the floe had revolved I could only guess. In any case, I now had to look for our camp in the west – if I was going to find it anywhere at all.

I busied myself digging the stang out of the stone-hard snowdrift. Without tools it was a murderous task. And things were about to get worse. I discovered that the entire brass surface of the ski was covered with a heavy crust of ice. I took my knife and scraped most of it off. However, an almost invisible layer of ice remained, making the thing almost impossible to use. It was like skiing on sand.

I finally gave up and began to walk westwards, dragging the stang behind me. Every now and again I'd stop and binocular-scan for the boat. But it was nowhere to be seen. Things were looking grim. What had happened in the storm? Where was I! Finally, with desperation really gripping me, I spied something tiny in the far distance. It grew slowly bigger. It was the boat!

As I made my way towards it my companions came out to meet me. Like me, the two younger men had been caught out by the storm but of course they'd had the small boat; they turned it over and sheltered inside. Our captain had headed back to the main boat as soon as he saw the weather turning. Their astonishment at my return was clear: all had thought me dead. Back at camp I wolfed down a huge meal and went to bed. I slept fourteen hours straight through!

# 12
# Kajaani

In 1919 my brother and I purchased Suvenniemi, an estate in central Finland. It lay just north of Kajaani in a region dominated by the huge Lake Oulu. The idea behind Suvenniemi was to establish Europe's first mink farm. A Norwegian who was bound for America to buy silver foxes was given the job of bringing back the necessary breeding stock. However, after he returned empty-handed – and very reluctantly gave back the cash – we abandoned the plan and decided to set up a zoological station breeding hares and various game birds, for which there was a big demand in Sweden. Alongside this we decided to trade in animals such as lynx, wolverines, bear cubs, otters, fresh-water seals, martens and moose. These we planned to acquire with the help of local hunters and sell to zoos and circuses. Through this I actually became the first lynx breeder in the world. It was pure luck. I just happened to put a single female with eight males. She became pregnant and gave birth to three healthy cubs. At once I realised that a female had to be attended by several males. To keep her with a single male was useless.

Our arrival at Kajaani was an episode in itself. It was a December evening and as our train pulled into the station we were informed that the body of water beyond which Suvenniemi lay wasn't yet frozen. At that time there was no road to the property, the only access being by boat in summer and across the ice in winter. We had three boxcars full of belongings, plus a motorboat, horse, raven, five ducks, a hound and a kitten, all being looked after by employee, Isak Erik. Our wives – Hans had married my wife's sister – were in Helsinki buying furniture.

What were we going to do now? We couldn't take the horse across in the boat, and even if we could, all the other stuff would take forever to ferry across. We left everything in the boxcars, took the kitten and wandered off to the only hotel in town. We were lucky: the hotel, which boasted only five rooms, had one free; it was ours if we didn't mind sharing.

We hadn't eaten all day and were starving. We ordered some food and were given a loaf of bread. It wasn't much but during the post-war period food was scarce and when we asked for more, we were told we'd had enough! We went to our room, but somehow the kitten slipped out and began playing in the hall. A forester, who was also staying in the hotel, discovered it and reported the matter to the hotel owner, enquiring who owned it.

'Oh, the kitten belongs to the new owners of Suvenniemi.'

Keen to meet these odd fellows who travelled with a cat, the forester came up to our room. As he entered I recognized him at once. His older sister had been in my class at high school. This changed things dramatically: the new owners of Suvenniemi had to be shown a proper welcome. Food and drink miraculously appeared and as the town folk gathered, a riotous celebration was soon in full swing. Well fed and watered, we didn't get to bed until the early hours.

In the morning we faced an extremely positive start to the day. During the night the temperature had dropped to below minus thirty and Erik, who had grown up around boats and ice, informed us it would be safe to undertake a test crossing. And he was right: we crossed the nine kilometres without incident.

'One more night like that and we can cross with horses,' he assured us. And sure enough the following day the proper transportation of our belongings began. Erik walked ahead with an axe, insisting that if the axe didn't go through the ice with one blow, it would support a horse. It was pretty nerve-wracking stuff because the current flowing out of the lake made the ice so thin in places that the axe went straight through, forcing us to find another route. However, by evening the entire contents of two boxcars had been shuttled across.

Our show of determination and bravery gained us immediate local approval – and friends. Daring was a trait admired by all, from the highest born to the poorest peasant. It was a leveler, an equalizer and our ice feat put us on a firm footing in our new home.

Kajaani was full of new experiences, and the first of these was served up that very first December. Every Christmas Kajaani held a huge market that had the town overflowing with incomers. The place was transformed into a mass of colour and activity and we wandered through it all simply mesmerised.

But we were also reminded of the still-lingering impact of all the political upheaval. In Russia things were still in turmoil and the Karelians on the other side of the border had nothing to eat. They arrived in town with their reindeer caravans to get flour, each animal able to pull a sledge carrying two sacks of the stuff. Just two men could handle a caravan of a hundred reindeer. The lead man would have a reindeer tied behind his sleigh with all the others following it. At the far end of the caravan the second man followed in his sleigh, overseeing the operation. They rested every second day to give the reindeer a chance to recover and browse on lichen. During this break the reindeer moved around at will, guarded only by dogs. This was also the case at night. It's a type of freedom that seems risky when the half-wild status of these animals is considered, but with their herd instinct keeping them together it worked perfectly – well, most of the time. When mushrooms began to appear in the autumn the reindeer would wander all over the place searching for what they clearly considered a delicacy. At such times herds would mix together and their owners had a devil of a time sorting them out.

Although all manner of things were sold and traded at the market, including horses, nothing matched the sale of pelts – otter, fox, marten, lynx, hare and squirrel. It was massive business with many hundreds of thousands changing hands. Sheep hides were also sold in vast quantities. The local sheep sported particularly fine wool and the grey fleeces were especially valuable.

Huge numbers of game birds were also on offer, piles of capercaillie, black grouse and pyramids of ptarmigan being displayed. The ptarmigan were all caught with snares: the exporters weren't interested in those that had been shot due to their feathers being bloodied. And they had to be pure white, something clearly stipulated by the main importer, Great Britain. (Sweden also took some, but the Germans didn't seem partial to them at all.)

The Kajaani of 1919 was indeed a world away from the modern bustling city of today. It was like a frontier town of the Old West or something from the Klondike gold rush. All its houses were made of wood and the main street had board walkways under which water tended to gather. Because the boards were flexible, a really wet spell would result in a vertical jet of water per stride! What the town's womenfolk thought of this I don't know!

The streets were surfaced with a kind of tough black clay, which, like the boardwalks, became a bit of a hazard in wet weather: they were so slippery you could hardly stand on them. I remember trying to cross to meet a friend and falling twice. At the third failed attempt I shouted across that we'd catch up when it stopped raining!

The market square was even worse. Its surface became a bouncy trampoline. Until it gave way! I recall one of the town's finer ladies sinking so deep she had to be dug out with a shovel. I believe her shoes were lost forever, perhaps to be found some day by an archaeologist.

Because nothing much happened in Kajaani, anything new was a source of great interest. So it was with the new forester. The old forester had died and a replacement was due. The local community was of course full of expectation, the arrival of someone new creating fever-pitch curiosity.

One day three horse-drawn loads arrived at the forestry office. Like wolves to a downed moose, everyone rushed over to meet the new forester. But disappointment: it was only items of furniture and household goods. However, not willing to let their enthusiasm be dampened, everyone got busy unloading and moving the goods inside – even arranging things according to their collective taste. Among the household goods were three little casks that aroused a great deal of interest. Northern folk have good noses and it didn't take long to come to the conclusion that the casks held cognac. Well, there they sat, house all furnished, guests all present and the required refreshment within reach. All that was needed was the host.

Another two carriages arrived. Again everyone hurried out to welcome the new forester, and again it turned out to be just supplies and household goods.

'Hmm,' said someone. 'I think it may be our duty to find out just what kind of man this new forester is. Didn't someone famous once say, "Show me your cognac and I'll tell you what kind of man you are?" I think it might have been Napoleon.'

'Yes,' said the policeman. 'And since I have to uphold the law I should definitely know what kind of man is coming to live amongst us.'

'Just open the tap,' said someone else who was becoming a bit impatient.

'Your will be done,' said the pastor, a bit slow on the draw as the liquid was already flowing.

A terrific celebration followed with everyone going through the various stages of drunkenness many times. On the second day the forester arrived and was hardly noticed. 'Who are you?' asked the policeman; and the pastor thought it was his nephew!

This weakness for the odd tipple had gossipmongers in the surrounding villages put it about that the inhabitants of Kajaani were constantly drunk. This was a lie. Heavy drinking sessions were not at all frequent, it's just that when they occurred they lasted for months! It made perfect sense. Stay drunk – it was the best way of avoiding a hangover!

It was said that alcohol had been the death of a retired dam-keeper. Again, a big lie. How could it have caused his death – he lived on nothing else! No one had seen him eat anything in years, though one old lady insisted she'd once seen him bite into a cucumber. Her eyesight was frightful: he was probably drinking from a bottle!

Like any small town, Kajaani had its share of characters, a memorable pile of the colourful and eccentric. Two such characters were brothers who played in amateur theatre productions. One night they visited a girl of dubious repute and managed to contract gonorrhoea. Despite the best efforts of the local doctor, the disease persisted.

Then one day one of them became seriously ill with influenza. When he recovered, the doctor discovered that he was also cured of his gonorrhoea and claimed that the very high fever must have killed it off. 'That's fantastic,' said the other, and lay down naked in a freezing room and managed to get pneumonia. The fever this created was well up to killing the gonorrhoea. The problem was it killed him too!

Another interesting figure was The Silent One. There are talkative and less talkative people in this world, but this fellow treated words as if they were gold. Some said he didn't say a word until he was seven and all assumed he couldn't speak. However, one fine harvest day, when it was hot and people were drinking buttermilk, he suddenly said, 'Me too.' Everyone was astonished and asked him why he hadn't spoken earlier. He quietly replied, 'I didn't have anything to say.'

I got to know this chap quite well and on one occasion accompanied him to a remote spot so he could collect some osprey eggs. He was a passionate egg collector. The nest – a huge thing – was at the top of an old pine and without a word he began to climb. It was no easy task as the lowest branches were far above ground. However, somehow he managed and was just about to remove the eggs when the branch he was on broke. He fell, but grabbed the tip of another branch below the nest. He just hung there and I could think of no way of helping him. After a while he said, 'I'm going to fall soon.' Then he said, 'I'm falling now.' And down he came, and broke his leg.

# 13
# The Åland Expedition

As our animal supply operation continued, the demand for live hares was enormous. In fact I couldn't nearly meet my orders: my attempts to breed them proved hit and miss and other sources were unreliable. I had to find a way of trapping them. In central Europe, brown hares have long been caught in field nets, a line of beaters driving them into the meshes. However, the mountain hare of Finland is a different animal inhabiting a different world. This is a creature of deep forest and one unwilling to be driven in a particular direction, running perhaps a hundred metres before curving left or right to end up behind those doing the driving. A very tight line might have been able to force the issue but men cost money and because this hare is not found in the densities of the brown hare, a drive perhaps yielding just a couple of hares, any captured animals would have been very expensive.

I decided to tackle the problem with hounds, using them just as I did with my eagles and gun: the hounds would get on a hare trail and push the animal along its own run right into a carefully placed net. To this end I had some special nets made: they were olive in colour, half a metre high, a hundred long and had a mesh size of six and a half centimetres. Rolled up, such a net could easily be carried by one man. And

they worked. By standing about twenty metres from the run, I found that as the hare came past I could actually drive it into the net, which then collapsed to envelop it. The hare was then placed in a dark basket to be transported home free of stress.

The tension and excitement involved made this type of hunting almost as enjoyable as hawking or shooting and Hans and I soon began to compete with one another, each taking out a helper to try and outdo the other. I recall scores of fifteen, but generally between five and eight hares were to be reckoned with, especially in the winter when the runs were much longer. As every hare was worth 225 Finnish Marks, it wasn't a bad business – and we quickly expanded. Young lads were lent nets and became independent trappers, selling their hares to us. Soon I was able to fill every order that came in.

That first success with hares was like the first drop of blood on the tooth of a kitten: it had to be possible to trap other animals in a similar manner. I frequently had inquiries for moose, but these were in short supply: I'd occasionally acquire a calf from Sweden, but Finnish ani-

mals less frequently came my way. What about netting? As far as I knew, nobody had ever attempted to live-trap moose, and certainly none of the books or publications I'd read mentioned it. Nevertheless, I decided to make an attempt.

Of course first I would need somewhere with high enough moose densities and where a year-round catch permit might be granted. There weren't many such places but I saw one definite possibility – Åland, an extensive range of islands lying off the southwest tip of Finland, almost slap bang between Finland and Sweden.

Åland was like an independent kingdom. It had been 'promised' to Finland in 1921 but was pretty much self-ruling and had its own government. It was a fascinating place, a land of immaculately kept houses, windmills and magnificent tall ships.* The climate was milder than mainland Finland and while pine, spruce and birch were dominant, other trees, such as oak, ash, alder, maple and rowan, not found in the rest of Finland, also grew.

*Remmler tells us that Åland was the last place on earth to have a fleet of tall ships. They sailed the waters between Europe and Australia carrying grain. It was an enterprise operated by the shipping company Eriksson and ran until World War Two.

Åland was home to lots of moose. They were a relatively new addition. Fifty years earlier they'd been unknown; then one day they just arrived! That moose are great swimmers is well documented. Ships have reported seeing them way out at sea between Finland and Sweden and I myself have seen a three-month-old calf enter the water and swim three kilometres to reach the next island. With Åland stretching quite close to the mainland, the eventual arrival of these animals was to be expected.

Åland's first moose were met with joy. However, as they became more numerous this joy cooled somewhat: the newcomers were destructive. By 1928 the damage to forest and flora was so extensive that something had to be done. It was a sensitive issue because despite the damage, residents considered the moose 'citizens of the islands' and didn't want them harmed. The authorities pretty much had their hands tied. Then my proposal arrived. Here was a way of removing the nuisance without pointing a gun at it, and I immediately got the go ahead. I could trap moose all year round and in any numbers I liked.

Now I had to come up with suitable nets. I sent samples of hemp, cotton and sisal rope to Helsinki University to be tested for strength. There was no nylon in those days. My final choice was sisal and it turned out to be perfect.

Each net was six metres high, fifty long and had a mesh size of sixty centimetres. One man could just about carry such a net. In total I had sixty nets made enabling me to cordon off an area of about three kilometres. The nets were designed to be suspended from branches by S-shaped wire hooks, the idea being that when a moose hit the net, the force would straighten the hook allowing the net to fall. Where less robust branches were used, it was presumed that these would simply break. I had a sail maker dye the nets green. Unfortunately the dye had quite a strong smell, which I'm sure hindered things somewhat.

So I had my nets. Now all I needed was a team of men to help me use them. My own full-time staff couldn't be spared, so I called on three hunter-trappers who frequently stepped in to help with all manner of things. Top man amongst these was a chap by the name of Mikkonen. Apart from being an expert trapper he was also a highly

skilled shoemaker. In fact given an axe and a knife he could produce just about anything, including skis. The two others were originally from Russian Karelia but had fled to Finland. The older one had served in the Russian army and had taken part in the first war. He'd travelled and seen a little of the wider world. The other was exactly the opposite. A true wilderness man, he'd never even walked a paved street.

In addition to my own men, I enlisted seven slightly less skilled assistants: all were more at home in the woods than the city and knew how to handle animals; they just weren't such finely tuned hunters. With this team, and Hans by my side, I felt pretty confident. We were ready to begin trapping.

In Marienhamn, Åland's only city and its capital, we were met with open arms and immediately rushed to the town hall for an audience with the mayor: a forester was put at our disposal and a journalist was going to follow our every move. There was however one small problem. Months earlier a newspaper had reported our planned visit and now there wasn't a soul in the archipelago who didn't want to take part. There was an army of thousands all ready to act as helpers and 'advisers'.

My intention had been to locate spots where small drives could be conducted, but my vast horde of helpers were having none of that. They wanted a giant drive where the whole population could take part and suggested we first comb through the forty square kilometre island of Lemland, which was connected to the main island by bridge. It was impossible to battle their insistence, so we loaded up our gear and set off.

That evening my team and I took a stroll from our accommodation and within minutes watched three moose step into the open, look leisurely in our direction and then proceed to munch the foliage of an aspen tree that had been browsed back to man-height. 'These Åland moose are going to be easy,' said Mikkonen. I decided to reserve judgement.

The islanders were now keen that I announce a date for the first drive, which I did. It was a bit of news that not only reached every corner of Åland, but also made every press office in northern Europe!

It even drew a film crew!

If I wasn't already sure that the whole thing was going to be a disaster, then what met me at the starting point of the drive certainly did. The crowd was enormous, a vast throng of bodies milling about like market day. Stories and jokes were being told, tittle-tattle exchanged – one man was even playing a harmonica! I arrived just as a fight broke out, a scuffle soon having two youths rolling about in the dirt, egged on by an appreciative audience. Their teacher assured me it was only a sign of growing up and excess adrenalin. My own starting to boil, I refrained from commenting. And all of this was diligently captured by the film crew.

Into the woods and much of the same continued, my efforts to hold my 'helpers' together in a straight line being a total waste of time. If left for just five minutes they would group together to chat and lark about – freely admitting that with so much disturbance all the moose would be long gone. One party, not too keen on 'all the branches', even took to the road!

It took about two hours to get to where the nets hung. My men informed me that just three moose had been spotted and all had taken to the water some way before the trap. But did this dampen the crowd's spirit? Not at all, they continued on to the village where a party was soon in full swing. But one thing had been achieved: seen as a total waste of time, no one was interested in coming out on any more netting expeditions. Now we could get down to work.

It hadn't rained for some time and the ground was hard. Thus, with moose tracks only visible on sandy soil and moors, it was difficult to tell what the animals' movements were. To get more information I bought some of the thinnest and cheapest twine I could find, a type that would break easily. I dyed it green and strung it in lines from tree to tree at chest height. Next morning we went out to inspect the lines; where they were broken, we knew a moose had passed. More than that, by noting the flow of the broken ends we were given the direction the animal was moving in. Using this system we soon had a clear picture of where moose were to be found and how best to set up square blocks of ground that could be driven.

Having decided where the main trails or runs were, we hung our nets, but rolled up the lower half so that the moose could continue travelling back and forth as before. We took our time and, still using the twine, made sure the moose would pass under the nets without paying attention to them. In total we had five main trails netted and now decided to drive one of the squares, a square our twine told us held at least one animal. The rolled up nets were dropped and flag lines were strung along two sides of the square so that it was closed on three sides. My brother and two of our team stayed by the nets, while I went with the beaters.

When I was within three hundred metres of the nets I spied three moose – a large bull, a cow and her calf – out on open ground. I hurried along, trying to encourage them into the nets. However, the bull shortly halted and turned around. I tried to chase him but, shaking his mighty antlers, he came straight for me. Yelling and waving my arms, I stood my ground but at the last second had to leap aside to escape being trampled. I could do nothing but watch all three of them trot away.

By now it was noon. We rolled up the flag lines and went back to our quarters for lunch. We left the nets down, planning to roll them up and see to any damaged twine later.

I was sitting with my brother when the phone rang. It was the owner of the neighbouring house. He had returned home an hour ago and seen a large bull entangled in one of the nets. I asked why he hadn't called sooner, and he replied that he'd wanted to finish eating first!

We made for the net as fast as possible but by the time we got there the moose was dead. I asked the neighbour if the bull had thrashed about much. 'No, he was just lying there like a horse would.'

The moose was cut up and divided amongst the families of the immediate area: the bigger your property the more moose you got. Our landlady's home was substantial, which soon introduced us to just how many ways moose can be cooked!

Two days later we drove another square. This time a two-year-old bull went into the nets. I was at the scene and able to watch what happened from beginning to end. As the net dropped, the moose rolled

once and stayed down, hardly moving; nor did he resist when his legs were tied. However, his breathing immediately became heavy and there was foam about his mouth. He was clearly in distress: eyes becoming redder and redder, breathing still heavier. Finally he laid his head down on the moss and died. From hitting the net to his sad end had taken just twenty minutes and we'd just stood there not knowing what to do.

I immediately halted trapping and sent telegrams and letters to several universities and veterinary schools inquiring about tranquillizers that might ease the stress of capture, the drugs in use today being unknown then. I was given a variety of suggestions – morphine, scopolamine, chloral and others – and we tried several, but the results were always the same: the moose died faster than before.

The situation was dire and I was on the verge of admitting defeat when I had an idea. So far we had trapped only adult moose. What about calves? Would these perhaps fare better?

I was still weighing up the idea when news came of an orphaned calf on the south end of Lemland Island. Its mother had died and it had remained close by. We immediately set off and hung nets right across the peninsular-like tip of the island. However, just as we were hanging the last net we watched the calf walk slowly into the water and swim in a big arc right around the nets. It took to the water so keenly that it must have done it before, possibly following its mother on a route that helped her avoid two nearby farms.

Now what? The nets were in the right place, but the calf was on the wrong side!

'Don't worry,' said Mikkonen. 'I'm sure the calf will be back.'

We walked to one of the farms to see if we could beg a cup of coffee. We were in luck but had hardly lifted our mugs when a young lad burst in excitedly informing us that the calf was in the nets.

Sure enough, there was the calf. We quickly tied its legs and took it gently over to the transport boat where it was laid on a bed of straw.

The journey back to our accommodation took three hours and involved both the boat and a horse cart. It was a terrifying ordeal – but apparently more for us than the calf, which, soon installed in a barn, began feeding without a care in the world!

We had now established that calves could be safely trapped, but before continuing, two things needed to be altered. Firstly, we needed enclosures near to the nets so that handling could be cut down; such enclosures would also do away with the need to move the moose immediately. Secondly, the net mesh had to be made smaller: it was just too big for calves. Both matters were time consuming but the nets proved especially so, requiring twelve men to untie the knots and retie them for a mesh size of about thirty centimetres square. It was a massive amount of work and took several weeks, but it couldn't be avoided.

The plan was of course to net only calves from now on, however I still wanted to try one last time with an adult to see if the newly built enclosures would help at all. It was a disaster. With watch in hand, I timed how long it took to move the moose from the net to the enclosure. Nine minutes exactly. We now stood back and observed from a distance. The moose stood still for a while, legs wide apart, his breathing heavy. Then the usual foam began to show around his mouth. He

then lay down, stretched his neck out and died. He lasted exactly twenty-one minutes in the enclosure, not making the slightest attempt to escape.

From that day on, every adult moose was chased away from the nets while the calves were allowed past to be driven into them. Things went well and we trapped a number of calves and kept them in the enclosures until they became trusting – which happens very quickly with young moose. Only then were they crated and shipped.

Eventually we reduced the calf population of Lemland so dramatically that I had to find a new trapping site and decided on Eckerö, the most westerly of the larger Åland islands.

Now winter was with us and the snow-covered ground made it much easier to follow what the moose were doing: there was no need for twine, their tracks told all. It immediately became clear that there weren't nearly as many moose as on Lemland, the far fewer deciduous trees and the rocky cliffs clearly keeping their numbers down.

We netted a few calves but as we went into February the old curse returned. We caught a calf that reacted very badly, demonstrating all the symptoms of stress seen in the adults. In spite of our best efforts it died within half an hour. It seemed the calves had reached a critical age – eight months – and were no longer able to deal with the stress.

With the death of the calf I ended trapping for that season, but our experiences on Åland were far from over. That night we decided to camp out rather than head back to base – and it was a wonderful night. We dressed the dead calf and roasted one of the quarters. The youngest of my Karelian hunter-trapper trio, Alexander Lesonen, had obviously developed a taste for moose and, working at twice our speed, ate most of the thing himself!

In the morning we woke to find the fire going again and Alex busy roasting the other quarter. As none of us were very hungry, he got to have most of it.

That evening he became ill and I took him to the hospital in Marienhamn. The doctors said it was liver failure and he was soon in such a bad way that I had his wife brought down from Kajaani. He was dead two days later.

We trapped moose for two years on the Åland Islands and as far as I know our experience remains unique: I don't think the islands have seen moose nets since.

# Epilogue

Remmler's time in Kajaani was one of the happiest periods of his life. He watched his children grow up enjoying the freedom of Suvenniemi and a second property, Syrjälä. He was also able to get back to eagle falconry, managing, with the help of full-time assistants, as many as sixteen birds. It was the period that gave him his wolf hawking and one that also saw many influential guests coming out to watch the eagles in action.

With this increasing fame came an invitation to the famous Berlin Hunting Exhibition of 1937. It was a massive event drawing visitors from all over the globe and Remmler travelled down with eagles and horses to entertain huge crowds – and the world press.

During this period Remmler was also working on a major film. An interest in scriptwriting had seen him associated with several minor productions, but this film – 'Bastard' – was a full-length feature. Set in the far north, the plot involved a fictitious tribe of nomads who rode reindeer and hunted wolves with golden eagles. Remmler wrote the script and handled all the animal training, using his own wolf-catching eagles for the hunting scenes. Released in 1940, Bastard won first prize at the Venice Film Festival.

War brought all of this to an end as the Remmler family entered a time of massive change and upheaval. A major complication was their German citizenship which, as Finland's relationship with Germany swung back and forth, caused all manner of problems: they were expelled, allowed back – expelled again! The only member of the family to avoid this turmoil was daughter Krimhild, who married a Finnish soldier and took Finnish citizenship.

During all of this, Remmler lost just about everything he owned: one property was bombed, another confiscated and all his eagles were shot. But a new beginning was about to dawn. Now based in Germany, in 1951 he was offered the position of gamekeeper-hunting guide on Griffiths Island in Lake Huron, Canada. He took the job and with Impi, Ingmar and eventually Orvar, emigrated.

Remmler remained on the island for thirteen years – not only attending to his employer's sporting requirements but his own, returning once again to golden eagles.

On his retirement, he and Impi moved to a farm on the Niagara River. Purchased with Ingmar, it allowed Remmler to continue working with his final eagles and do a little film work – which resulted in the award winning 'The Bear and the Mouse'. It was here too that he penned his lost manuscript. He died of a heart attack on October 18, 1972.

# Further Reading

## *The last Wolf Hawker*

### *The Eagle Falconry of Friedrich Remmler*

Martin Hollinshead

'The most complete picture to date of the fascinating and influential Remmler.' *Hawk Chalk*

'From Remmler's vivid hunt accounts, I can feel the whole atmosphere: the landscape, the baying of the hounds as the quarry draws nearer, and finally the flight and kill ... I heartily recommend this book.'
*The Austringer*

'A real gem of a book ... one I could read over and over again.' *The Falconers & Raptor Conservation Magazine*

'Martin Hollinshead rediscovers the legendary eagle pioneer, and adds to his story the analytical perspective of someone who hunts with eagles. Anyone interested in eagles should not miss this book.'
*Stephen Bodio, Author and Falconer*

Published by The Fernhill Press 2006